GCSE Bitesize

D0527700

Religious Studies

Complete Revision and Practice

Jon Mayled

P   , BBC Active, an imprint of Educational Publishers LLP, part of the Pearson Education Group Edinburgh Gate,
H   CM 20 2JE, England

T   © Jon Mayled/BBC Worldwide Ltd, 2004, 2008, 2010

C   cent copyright © BBC Worldwide Ltd, 2002, 2004/BBC Active 2008, 2010

B   BC 1996. BBC and BBC Active are trademarks of the British Broadcasting Corporation

T   Mayled to be identified as the author of this Work have been asserted by him in accordance with
th   Designs and Patents Act, 1988.

IS   5446-2

P   SC/01

Th   olicy is to use paper manufactured from sustainable forests.

Fi   2002

Ti   10

LS 1636a recommended system requirements
          ws(r), XP sp2, Pentium 4 1 GHz processor (2 GHz for Vista), 512 MB of RAM (1 GB for Windows Vista), 1 GB of free hard disk
space, CD-ROM drive 16x, 16 bit colour monitor set at 1024 x 768 pixels resolution
MAC: Mac OS X 10.3.9 or higher, G4 processor at 1 GHz or faster, 512 MB RAM, 1 GB free space (or 10% of drive capacity, whichever
is higher), Microsoft Internet Explorer® 6.1 SP2 or Macintosh Safari™ 1.3, Adobe Flash® Player 9 or higher, Adobe Reader® 7 or higher,
Headphones recommended

If you experiencing difficulty in launching the enclosed CD-ROM, or in accessing content, please review the following notes:
1 Ensure your computer meets the minimum requirements. Faster machines will improve performance.
2 If the CD does not automatically open, Windows users should open 'My Computer', double-click on the CD icon, then the file named
'launcher.exe'. Macintosh users should double-click on the CD icon, then 'launcher.osx'
Please note: the eDesktop Revision Planner is provided as-is and cannot be supported.
For other technical support, visit the following address for articles which may help resolve your issues:
http://centraal.uk.knowledgebox.com/kbase/

If you cannot find information which helps you to resolve your particular issue, please email: Digital.Support@pearson.com.
Please include the following information in your mail:
- Your name and daytime telephone number.
- ISBN of the product (found on the packaging.)
- Details of the problem you are experiencing
- Details of your computer (operating system, F

XB00 000006 8826

Contents

* Only available in the CD-ROM version of the book.

Exam board specification map

Provides a quick and easy overview of the topics you need to study for the examinations you will be taking.

Topics	Page	AQA A	AQA B	CCEA	Edexcel	OCR A	OCR B	WJEC A	WJEC B
Central beliefs									
The nature of God and the Trinity	2	✓	✓	✓	✓	✓	✓	✓	✓
The Bible	4	✓	✓	✓	✓	✓	✓	✓	✓
Jesus	6	✓	✓	✓	✓	✓	✓	✓	✓
The Ten Commandments	8	✓	✓	✓	✓	✓	✓	✓	✓
The Sermon on the Mount	10	✓	✓	✓	✓	✓	✓	✓	✓
The problem of evil	12	✓	✓	✓	✓	✓	✓	✓	✓
History and Christian life									
The church – history	14	✓	✓	✓	✓	✓		✓	
Christian denominations	16	✓	✓	✓	✓	✓	✓	✓	✓
Ecumenism	18	✓	✓	✓	✓	✓	✓	✓	✓
The church – buildings and features	20	✓	✓	✓		✓	✓	✓	✓
Pilgrimage	22	✓	✓	✓	✓	✓	✓	✓	✓
Prayer	24	✓	✓	✓	✓	✓	✓	✓	✓
Sacraments									
Baptism	26	✓	✓	✓	✓	✓	✓	✓	✓
The Eucharist	28	✓	✓	✓	✓	✓	✓	✓	✓
Confirmation	30	✓	✓	✓	✓	✓	✓	✓	✓
Funerals	32	✓	✓	✓	✓	✓	✓	✓	✓
Life after death	34	✓	✓	✓	✓	✓	✓	✓	✓
Holy days									
The Christian year	36	✓	✓	✓	✓	✓		✓	
Advent and Christmas	38	✓	✓	✓	✓	✓		✓	
Lent, Holy Week and Easter	40	✓	✓	✓	✓	✓		✓	
Ascension and Pentecost	42	✓	✓	✓	✓	✓		✓	
Wealth and poverty									
Care for the poor	44	✓	✓	✓	✓	✓	✓	✓	✓
Christian aid organisations	46	✓	✓	✓	✓	✓	✓	✓	✓
Christian attitudes to money and wealth	48	✓	✓	✓	✓	✓	✓	✓	✓

Introduction

How to use GCSE Bitesize Complete Revision and Practice

Begin with the CD-ROM. There are five easy steps to using the CD-ROM – and to creating your own personal revision programme. Follow these steps and you'll be fully prepared for the exam without wasting time on areas you already know.

Topic checker

Step 1: Check

The Topic checker will help you figure out what you know – and what you need to revise.

Revision planner

Step 2: Plan

When you know which topics you need to revise, enter them into the handy Revision planner. You'll get a daily reminder to make sure you're on track.

Step 3: Revise

From the Topic checker, you can go straight to the topic pages that contain all the facts you need to know.

- Give yourself the edge with the Web*Bite* buttons. These link directly to the relevant section on the BBC Bitesize Revision website.

- Audio*Bite* buttons let you listen to more about the topic to boost your knowledge even further. *

Step 4: Practise

Check your understanding by answering the Practice questions. Click on each question to see the correct answer.

Step 5: Exam

Are you ready for the exam? Exam*Bite* buttons take you to an exam question on the topics you've just revised. *

* Not all subjects contain these features, depending on their exam requirements.

About this book

Use this book whenever you prefer to work away from your computer.
It consists of two main parts:

 A set of double-page spreads, covering the essential topics for revision from each of the curriculum areas. Each topic is organised in the following way:

- A summary of the main points and an introduction to the topic.

- Lettered section boxes cover the important areas within each topic.

- Key facts are clearly highlighted – these indicate the essential information in a section or give you tips on answering exam questions.

- Practice questions at the end of each topic – a range of questions to check your understanding.

 A number of special sections to help you consolidate your revision and get a feel for how exam questions are structured and marked. These extra sections will help you check your progress and be confident that you know your stuff. They include:

- A selection of exam-style questions and worked model answers and comments to help you get full marks.

- Topic checker – quick questions covering all topic areas.

- Complete the facts – check that you have the most important ideas at your fingertips.

- Last-minute learner – the most important facts in just a few pages.

About your exam

Get organised
You need to know when your exams are before you make your revision plan. Check the dates, times and locations of your exams with your teacher, tutor or school office.

On the day
Aim to arrive in plenty of time, with everything you need: several pens, pencils, a ruler, and possibly mathematical instruments, a calculator, or a language dictionary, depending on the exam subject.

On your way or while you're waiting, read through your Last-minute learner.

In the exam room
When you are issued with your exam paper, you must not open it immediately. However, there are some details on the front cover that you can fill in (your name, centre number, etc.) before you start the exam itself. If you're not sure where to write these details, ask one of the invigilators (teachers supervising the exam).

When it's time to begin writing, read each question carefully. Remember to keep an eye on the time.

Finally, don't panic! If you have followed your teacher's advice and the suggestions in this book, you will be well-prepared for any question in your exam.

Topic checker

 Go through these questions after you've revised a group of topics, putting a tick if you know the answer.

 You can check your answers on pages xiv–xvii.

>> Central beliefs

1   Who are the three 'persons' of the Trinity?

2   What are the two sections of the Bible?

3   Where was Jesus born?

4   Who were Jesus' mother and father?

5   Who was given the Ten Commandments?

6   Name three of the Ten Commandments.

7   Who preached the Sermon on the Mount?

8   What are the Beatitudes?

9   Who was Paul?

10   Explain what is meant by 'the problem of evil'.

11   What does the Book of Job teach about suffering?

12   What is the difference between 'moral evil' and 'natural evil'?

>> History and Christian life

13   What are the three main divisions of the Church?   ☐

14   Who is the Pope?   ☐

15   Why is the Patriarch of Constantinople important?   ☐

16   Name two non-Conformist churches.   ☐

17   What does ecumenism mean?   ☐

18   What is the World Council of Churches?   ☐

19   What is a font?   ☐

20   Why is the altar important in many churches?   ☐

21   What is the pulpit used for?   ☐

22   What is a pilgrimage?   ☐

23   Where might Christians go on pilgrimage?   ☐

24   Name three types of prayer.   ☐

25   Name two well-known prayers.   ☐

Topic checker

>> Sacraments

26 What happens at a baptism?

27 What is Original Sin?

28 Why do some people get confirmed?

29 What are the vows in a marriage ceremony?

30 What do Christians believe about life after death?

31 What is purgatory?

>> Holy days

32 What is Advent?

33 Why is Christmas such an important festival for Christians?

34 What does Lent recall?

35 What happened during Holy Week?

36 What happened on Easter Sunday?

37 What was the Ascension?

38 What happened at the first Pentecost?

>> Wealth and poverty

Topic checker

39   What did the prophet Amos teach about how people should treat the poor?

40   Give three examples of work a Christian aid organisation might do in a developing country.

41   What is the parable of the rich man and Lazarus about?

42   Give three examples of occupations that a Christian might consider to be wrong ways of earning money.

43   What is the parable of the sheep and the goats about?

>> Medical ethics

44   What is meant by the phrase 'the sanctity of life'?

45   Name an organisation Christians might support, which helps people who are thinking of committing suicide.

46   What is meant by 'passive euthanasia'?

47   Why might some Christians be in favour of euthanasia?

48   What do Roman Catholics believe about the use of contraception?

49   Give an example of Christian teaching that might be used to support the view that abortion is wrong.

50   Give three things a Christian might do to put into practice the belief that abortion is wrong.

51   Why might some Christians be in favour of embryo research?

52   What does IVF stand for?

53   Why might some Christians be against fertility treatment?

54   What is Dame Cicely Saunders famous for?

Topic checker

55   What opinion would you expect a member of the Religious Society of Friends to have about whether it is right to fight in a war? ☐

56   What is a 'conscientious objector'? ☐

57   Who set down the conditions necessary for a Just War? ☐

58   Name an organisation Christians might support, which helps the victims of human rights abuses. ☐

59   In which book of the Bible does it say that people were created in the image of God? ☐

60   Why might some Christians be in favour of capital punishment? ☐

61   Which parable told by Jesus illustrates the point that everyone should be treated as a neighbour, whatever their race? ☐

62   What was Martin Luther King Jr.'s 'I have a dream' speech about? ☐

63   What was apartheid? ☐

64   What is Trevor Huddleston famous for? ☐

>> Family, relationships and gender

65 What do Roman Catholics believe about divorce? ☐

66 What does the Church of England teach about divorce? ☐

67 What Biblical teaching might a Christian use to support the view that men should have a leadership role in the home and in church? ☐

>> Global issues

68 In which book of the Bible does it say that people are to be the stewards of the earth? ☐

69 Name an organisation that a Christian might choose to support, which aims to help conserve and protect the environment. ☐

70 Give three ways in which a Christian might show concern for the environment. ☐

71 Why might some Christians disagree with scientific theories about the way the world began? ☐

72 Name a scientist famous for developing the theory of evolution and the theory of natural selection. ☐

Topic checker answers

>> Central beliefs

1	God the Father, God the Son, God the Holy Spirit
2	Old Testament, New Testament
3	Bethlehem
4	Mary and Joseph (earthly father) or God (real father)
5	Moses
6	**1** You shall have no other gods **2** You shall not worship idols **3** You shall not misuse the name of God **4** Remember the Sabbath day and keep it holy **5** Honour your father and mother **6** You shall not murder **7** You shall not commit adultery **8** You shall not steal **9** You shall not give false testimony against your neighbour **10** You shall not covet (be envious of) your neighbour's possessions
7	Jesus
8	The first section of the Sermon on the Mount, beginning, 'Blessed are... '
9	A Jew who had a vision that Jesus called him. He began to preach the message of Christianity throughout the Mediterranean.
10	It means the problems raised by the existence of evil and suffering in the world, because this suggests that there cannot be a God who is all-loving and all-powerful (omnipotent).
11	It teaches that suffering should be accepted with patience and faith, and that people should not expect to understand what God chooses to do.
12	Moral evil is the wrong caused by human wickedness, such as murder or violence. Natural evil is suffering caused by nature, such a disease, drought or earthquake.

>> History and Christian life

13	Orthodox, Roman Catholic, Protestant
14	He is head of the Roman Catholic Church.
15	He is head of the Orthodox Church.
16	There are many you could choose: Baptist, Methodist and United Reformed are examples.
17	Ecumenism is the name given to the belief that all churches should try to become more united. It is a movement that encourages Christians to worship together and forget their differences.
18	The World Council of Churches was formed after the Second World War, in 1948, by Christians who wanted to do something about restoring peace in the world. The WCC promotes ecumenism by encouraging Christians to work more closely together.
19	A bowl that holds the water for baptism.
20	Because the Eucharist is celebrated there.

21 For preaching and sometimes for reading the Bible.

22 A journey to a special place usually associated with a religion.

23 There are many you could choose: Rome, Lourdes, Walsingham and the Holy Land are examples.

24 Petitionary prayer is when people ask God for something, for themselves or for other people. Intercessory prayer is when people ask God to intervene in the world at a time of crisis or when people are starving or suffering because of a disaster. Prayers to give thanks.

25 Lord's Prayer, Hail Mary, Jesus Prayer

>> Sacraments

26 The sign of the cross is made on the baby's forehead with water and he or she is blessed in the 'Name of the Father, the Son and the Holy Spirit'.

27 Christians believe that, because of the disobedience of Adam and Eve in the garden of Eden, all people are born with Original Sin. This sin needs to be removed before people can truly live their lives as Christians.

28 They choose to make promises to God themselves to live a Christian life.

29 The promises that the couple make to each other and to God.

30 Christians believe that when they die they will have the chance of eternal life. Christians believe that they may go to heaven, hell or purgatory, depending on how well they have lived on earth.

31 Some Christians believe that most people are probably not good enough to go straight to heaven because of sins they have committed on earth, but they have believed in Jesus so they will not go to hell. Instead, they are taken to purgatory where they are punished for a period of time before they are able to enter heaven.

>> Holy days

32 The four weeks of preparation before Christmas.

33 Because it celebrates the incarnation, the birth of Jesus.

34 The 40 days that Jesus spent in the wilderness after his baptism.

35 Jesus preached in Jerusalem and ate the Last Supper with his disciples.

36 Jesus rose from the dead.

37 The time when Jesus finally left his disciples and went up to heaven.

38 The disciples received the gift of the Holy Spirit.

>> Wealth and poverty

39 He taught that the poor should be treated with justice; he taught that God would punish those who were unkind to the poor.

Topic checker answers

40	There are many examples you could use including: providing emergency relief such as food, shelter and medicines in times of disaster; providing clean water; giving health education; teaching literacy skills; supporting fair trade; helping people to learn new skills; supporting women's co-operatives.
41	It says that it is wrong to ignore the poor.
42	There are many examples you could choose: jobs that depend on pornography, gambling, drugs, alcohol or tobacco, prostitution, crime, etc.
43	It teaches that whatever people do to care for each other, they are doing it for Jesus, and when they ignore people in need, they ignore Jesus. They will be judged according to how they treat others.

>> Medical ethics

44	It means the holiness of life – it shows the belief that all life is given by God and is special.
45	The Samaritans
46	It means that someone's life ends because treatment that could have helped him or her to live longer is not given, so that death comes more quickly.
47	They might believe that it is the kindest way to help someone in pain. They might try to treat the person in the way that they would like to be treated themselves if they had a painful illness or serious disability.
48	They believe that only natural methods should be used, not artificial.
49	There are many examples you could use: perhaps Psalm 139 ('you knew me before I was born'), or Exodus 20:13 ('do not murder').
50	They might use their vote to support anti-abortion campaigns; go on a march; lobby their MP; join a letter-writing campaign; work for an adoption agency; support an organisation such as Life or the Society for the Protection of Unborn Children.
51	They might believe that it provides an opportunity for discovering more about curing serious illnesses, and therefore it is a loving thing to do. They might argue that Jesus was a healer. They might say that the embryos used would have been wasted otherwise, and this helps some good to come out of abortion.
52	In Vitro Fertilisation (fertilisation in glass)
53	They might believe that it interferes with God's plans for that couple. They might be worried about it being used for people who would not naturally have children, such as homosexual couples or women beyond the natural age for childbirth. They might worry about what happens to spare embryos. They might be concerned that AID introduces a third adult into a married relationship.
54	She promoted the modern hospice movement in the UK, to provide care for the dying.

>> War, peace and justice

55	They are likely to be pacifists and choose not to fight.
56	It is someone who objects to fighting in a war because his or her conscience says that war is wrong.

57 Thomas Aquinas

58 Amnesty International

59 Genesis

60 They might believe that it shows justice. Capital punishment is recommended in the Bible for some crimes. They might think it is kinder to the victim and their family to prevent the criminal from ever repeating the crime. They might think it is more humane than a life sentence.

61 The parable of the Good Samaritan

62 It was about his dream for the future, when black and white people would live together peacefully and equally.

63 It was a system in South Africa which made it illegal for black and white people to mix. It gave many rights and privileges to white people, and very few to black people.

64 He was a Christian priest who fought against apartheid.

>> Family, relationships and gender

65 They believe that marriage is a sacrament and is for life, and so they do not recognise divorce.

66 It teaches that ideally marriage should be for life, but it recognises divorce. Divorced people can be remarried in church as long as the vicar agrees.

67 Possibly 1 Timothy 2:9–12 ('wives behave modestly and submit to your husbands'), or Titus 2:5 ('wives be busy at home and submit to your husbands').

>> Global issues

68 Genesis

69 There are many you could choose: Greenpeace, the World Wide Fund for Nature or Friends of the Earth are examples.

70 There are many examples you could choose, including: recycling, using less packaging, using public transport, economising on fuel, lobbying MPs on environmental issues, joining a conservation group.

71 They might believe that the Biblical account of creation, given in Genesis, is literally true, and it does not match scientific theories.

72 Charles Darwin, Alfred Wallace

The nature of God and the Trinity

- Christians are monotheists, which means that they believe there is only one God.

- Christians believe that this one God has three different 'persons' or 'natures': God the Father, God the Son and God the Holy Spirit. These three persons together are known as the Trinity.

A What is the Trinity?

1 The **Trinity** is the way in which Christians describe God and can understand what God is.

The **God** of Christianity **has three 'persons' or 'natures'.** These three are different but they are all part of the same God.

Christians say that the idea of the Trinity is found in the Bible where God is described in different ways. **The Creeds** of the Christian Church, such as the Apostles' Creed and the Nicene Creed, **describe the Trinity.**

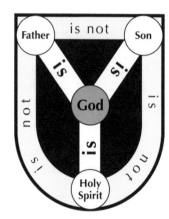

>> **key fact** The Trinity is the idea that there are three persons who are all God, not three Gods.

2 The three persons of the Trinity:

God the Father is seen as the **creator** of the universe. The title Father is also used as a way of showing human dependence on God in a close and loving relationship.

God the Son is Jesus. Christians believe that Jesus was **God in human form** and not just an ordinary man. Christians also believe that the death and resurrection of Jesus made it possible for them to have salvation.

God the Holy Spirit is **the way in which God lives in the hearts and lives of believers.** Christians believe that, after the Ascension (see p.43), God sent the Holy Spirit to comfort and guide people.

remember >>

Christians believe that Jesus was a human being but he was also God.

2

B The nature of God

Christians believe that God has several attributes:

Omnibenevolence – God is all good

Omnipotence – God is all powerful

Omnipresence – God is present everywhere at the same time

Omniscience – God knows everything

Transcendence – God is outside of time and space

Immanence – God is in everything.

- Christians also believe that God will **judge everyone** at the end of time and that God **created the universe for a purpose**.

- Sometimes people talk about God as being impersonal and mysterious. God is then seen as a sort of **force for good**. On other occasions people see God as very personal, like **a friend** who is concerned about your needs and feelings.

- The Alpha and Omega symbol is a name used for God in the Book of Revelation:

> I am the Alpha and the Omega, the Beginning and the End. (Revelation 21:6).

- Alpha and Omega are the first and last letters of the classical Greek alphabet.

C Alternative ideas about God

In recent years, people have begun to refer to God as a mother as well as a father. Traditionally, God has been seen as a man but the Bible says that **God created human beings in his image** and therefore many women have said that **God should be thought of as female as well as male**.

>> practice questions

1 **What do Christians mean by the Trinity?**

2 **Explain why some people believe that God should be thought of as a mother as well as a father.**

3 **Which attribute of God do you think is the most important? Give reasons for your view.**

The Bible

- The Bible is the most important and holy book in Christianity.

- Christians believe that the Bible is the revealed 'Word of God', and one of the ways in which God communicates to humanity.

- Christians try to understand the teachings of the Bible and to put them into practice in their daily lives.

A What is the Bible?

- The Christian scriptures which contain the Old Testament and the New Testament, are called the Bible.

- The **Old Testament** contains 39 books which together make up the whole of the Jewish Bible – the Tenakh. Jews refer to the first five books of their scriptures – Genesis, Exodus, Leviticus, Numbers and Deuteronomy – as the Torah (law). They believe that these books were given directly to Moses by God.

- The **New Testament** is the collected writings of some of the first Christians. The New Testament contains teachings about the life and death of Jesus, and about what it means to be a Christian. The 27 individual books of the New Testament were probably written in the first hundred years after the death of Jesus, but were not brought together until 367CE.

B What do Christians believe about the Bible?

- Christians believe that the Bible is a sacred text and is the revealed 'Word of God': revealed by God to humans. However, they may disagree about the literal truth of what it says.

- Some Christians believe that the Bible is literally true and that everything in the Bible happened in exactly the way that it is described. They believe that if scientists or historians have a different understanding of the world, it is the Bible which is right and people who are wrong, because they think that people make mistakes but God never does.

- These Christians are often called '**fundamentalists**' or '**creationists**'. They might have difficulties when passages in the Bible seem to be contradicted by modern evidence.

- Other Christians believe that parts of the Bible are not literally true, but are true in other ways, perhaps as stories that teach important things about life. They may also believe that, sometimes, the Bible displays an understanding of the world that is outdated now.

>> **key fact**   Christians believe that the Bible is the Word of God. Some people believe every word of the Bible is the literal truth while others believe that it has to be interpreted because it can sometimes be out-of-date.

Old Testament

- **Jesus was a Jew**, as were his followers. For this reason, the Old Testament is very important to Christians and Jews.

- It contains history, law, poetry and prophecy.

- One of its major themes is the relationship between God and humanity. The prophets wrote about the coming of a **Messiah**, who would bring peace to the earth.

- Isaiah wrote about a **Servant of God** who would suffer for the people's sins. Christians believe that this servant was Jesus.

New Testament

- The first four books are the **Gospels** of Matthew, Mark, Luke and John. Gospels mean 'good news' The Gospels are about the main events in the **life of Jesus**.

- The next book is the **Acts of the Apostles**.

- There are 21 books which are called the **Epistles**, or letters.

- The final book of the New Testament is the Apocalypse or **Book of Revelation** and it is a book of prophecy about what will happen during the last days of the world.

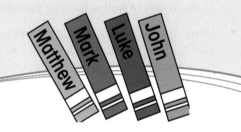

Many Christians read some of the Bible every day. They use it as a guide when making important decisions and as a comfort in difficult times. Christians use the Bible as a tool for worship during church services.

remember >>

The Bible is in two parts, the Old Testament and the New Testament, and it is the New Testament which is about Jesus and his teachings.

>> practice questions

1 **What do Christians believe about the Bible?**

2 **Explain what is meant by the Old and New Testaments.**

Jesus

The life of Jesus is an essential part of the Christian faith and there are a number of key events which are very important.

Christians believe that Jesus was the Son of God.

A Who was Jesus?

>> **key fact** Christians believe that Jesus Christ was the Son of God. They believe that Jesus was God incarnate, which means God in human form.

- They also believe that God came to the Earth as a man to live amongst other people, to teach them and to share in their sufferings.

- Jesus was probably born sometime between 8 and 3BCE, in the town of Bethlehem in Judaea, Palestine.

- Jesus' mother was a young woman, called Mary. His father was a carpenter, called Joseph, but although Joseph was responsible for bringing up the young boy, the Bible teaches that his real father was God.

- We know very little about Jesus until he was aged about 30. He visited his cousin, John the Baptist, and was **baptized** by him. It was then that his work started and his followers began to believe that Jesus was the Son of God.

study hint >>

Jesus' mother was Mary but his father was God.

remember >>

Almost everything we know about Jesus took place in the three years before he died.

B What did Jesus do?

- After his Baptism, **Jesus went into the wilderness for 40 days** to prepare himself for his ministry. Here he was tempted unsuccessfully by the Devil who offered Jesus riches and power if he would follow him rather than God.

- After this, Jesus gathered around him a group of men who are known as the **Twelve Disciples**. These were all working men from Galilee: Simon Peter, Andrew, John, Philip, James the son of Zebedee, Bartholomew, Thomas, Matthew, James the son of Alphaeus, Thaddaeus, Simon and Judas Iscariot.

- Jesus **preached** in the open and attracted enormous crowds wherever he went. He performed many **miracles** during his ministry in Galilee, in particular healing the sick and the lame and making the blind see.

- Most of his teaching was in **parables**. These were stories which his listeners could easily understand, but which had a very important message. A good example is the famous story of the Good Samaritan (Luke 10: 29–37).

C The crucifixion of Jesus

- Jesus angered the Jewish authorities with his teaching and the Jewish priests were alarmed by the claim that Jesus was the **Messiah**. They expected the Messiah to be a king leading an army to free them from the rule of the Romans and Jesus was nothing at all like this, being a poor carpenter.

- At the time of the feast of the Passover, Jesus celebrated a special meal with his disciples, **the Last Supper**. He was betrayed to the soldiers of the High Priest by **Judas Iscariot**. The High Priest and the elders (the Sanhedrin) tried Jesus and he was then taken before **Pontius Pilate**, the Roman Governor.

- Pilate was reluctant to execute Jesus but the Jewish priests were so insistent on his guilt that Pilate was finally forced to sentence him to death. **Jesus was crucified on what became known as Good Friday.**

- A rich follower of Jesus, Joseph of Arimathea, had Jesus' body taken away and placed in a private tomb. The Sabbath began that evening, so it was not until Sunday morning that anyone could visit the tomb.

- When three women arrived at the tomb on Sunday they found that the stone covering the entrance had been rolled away. At first, they thought someone had stolen the body but, shortly afterwards, they met Jesus. **He had risen from the dead**.

- Jesus met with his disciples and other followers, and ate and talked with them for another 40 days. Then he was taken up into heaven and they did not see him on earth again.

- When Jesus' disciples gathered together to celebrate the festival of **Pentecost** they received the Holy Spirit. This appeared as tongues of flame over them and they found that they could speak in different languages so that they could spread the teachings of Jesus.

study hint >>

Jesus was a Jew, not a Christian.

 **key fact** Jesus was a man, but he was also God.

>> practice questions

1 **What was special about the birth of Jesus?**

2 **What important teaching is found in the parable of the Good Samaritan?**

The Ten Commandments

A What are the Ten Commandments?

The Ten Commandments are found in several places in the Old Testament, including Exodus 20.

Three months after the Israelites escaped from Egypt and were wandering in the desert; God called Moses to the top of Mount Sinai and gave him two stone tablets on which were written the Ten Commandments.

You shall have no other gods.	You shall not worship idols.	You shall not misuse the name of God.	Remember the Sabbath day and keep it holy.	Honour your father and mother.
You shall not murder.	You shall not commit adultery.	You shall not steal.	You shall not give false testimony against your neighbour.	You shall not covet (be envious of) your neighbour's possessions.

study hint >>

Jesus said he did not want to change the Ten Commandments in any way.

B What do they mean?

The first four commandments are about **how people should behave towards God**. The other six commandments are about **how people should treat each other**. For both Jews and Christians, all of the commandments are equally important.

C Why are the Ten Commandments important?

>> **key fact** **The Ten Commandments are part of the 'covenant', or agreement, made between God and humanity.**

- The Ten Commandments were given by God to Moses as a set of **rules to live by**. They apply to everyone, all of the time.

- If people obeyed these rules, God would be pleased with them and take care of them.

- If people disobeyed the rules, then God would punish them. There are several examples in the Old Testament of people being punished for breaking some of the commandments.

In Exodus 21, God gives rules about punishments:

> Anyone who strikes a man and kills him shall surely be put to death…Anyone who attacks his father or his mother must be put to death. Anyone who kidnaps another and either sells him or still has him when he is caught must be put to death. Anyone who curses his father or mother must be put to death.
> (Exodus 21: 12, 15–17)

study hint >>

The Ten Commandments are just as important for Christians today as they were for the Israelites in the desert.

There is another occasion when someone breaks the rule about not working on the Sabbath:

> While the Israelites were in the desert, a man was found gathering wood on the Sabbath day. Those who found him gathering wood brought him to Moses and Aaron and the whole assembly, and they kept him in custody, because it was not clear what should be done to him. Then the Lord said to Moses, 'The man must die. The whole assembly must stone him outside the camp.' So the assembly took him outside the camp and stoned him to death, as the Lord commanded Moses.
> (Leviticus 15:32–36)

>> **key fact** Many of our laws today are still based on the Ten Commandments.

- In synagogues and also in many churches the Ten Commandments are written on the walls so that people are always reminded that these were the laws which God gave to humanity and which all people must keep in order to obey God.

>> **key fact** Jews and Christians believe that these rules apply to everyone all the time. They give us an outline of the right way to live.

study hint >>

Jesus said that the two greatest commandments were 'to love God and to love your neighbour as yourself'. Although these are not part of the original Ten Commandments, they do, in fact, summarise them.

>> practice questions

1. Why do you think God gave his people the Ten Commandments?
2. Explain why the fourth commandment to remember the Sabbath day and keep it holy, is important.

The Sermon on the Mount

- Jesus delivered a sermon, usually called the Sermon on the Mount, when he was near to the Sea of Galilee (Matthew 5–7).

- During this sermon he taught people the Beatitudes and the Lord's Prayer.

A What are the Beatitudes?

remember >>

The Beatitudes are just the first part of the Sermon on the Mount.

The Beatitudes

Blessed are the poor in spirit, for theirs is the kingdom of heaven.

Blessed are those who mourn, for they will be comforted.

Blessed are the meek, for they will inherit the earth.

Blessed are those who hunger and thirst for righteousness, for they will be filled.

Blessed are the merciful, for they will be shown mercy.

Blessed are the pure in heart, for they will see God.

Blessed are the peacemakers, for they will be called sons of God.

Blessed are those who are persecuted because of righteousness, for theirs is the kingdom of heaven.

Blessed are you when people insult you, persecute you and falsely say all kinds of evil against you because of me. Rejoice and be glad, because great is your reward in heaven, for in the same way, they persecuted the prophets who were before you. (Matthew 5:3–12)

>> key fact Jesus explained that although people often had to suffer in their lives on earth, God loved them and they would be rewarded and comforted when they died and went to heaven.

B What is the Lord's Prayer?

Jesus said people often made a great fuss about praying, and prayed in public so other people would see them and see how holy they were. He said that this was wrong and told people that they should pray using the Lord's Prayer.

Our Father in heaven, hallowed be your name,
your kingdom come,
your will be done
on earth as it is in heaven.
Give us today our daily bread.
Forgive us our debts,
as we also have forgiven our debtors.
And lead us not into temptation,
but deliver us from the evil one.
(Matthew 6:9–13)

study hint >>

Jesus said the Lord's Prayer was the one prayer which people needed.

C What other teachings are in the Sermon on the Mount?

1 Jesus taught people not to judge others.

> Do not judge, or you too will be judged. For in the same way as you judge others, you will be judged, and with the measure you use, it will be measured to you. (Matthew 7:1–2)

2 He taught that adultery and divorce were wrong.

> It has been said, 'Anyone who divorces his wife must give a certificate of divorce'. But I tell you that anyone who divorces his wife, except for marital unfaithfulness, causes her to become an adultress, and anyone who marries the divorced woman commits adultery. (Matthew 5:43–45)

3 He also taught that people should forgive others.

> You have heard that it was said, 'Love your neighbour and hate your enemy'. But I tell you: Love your enemies and pray for those who persecute you, that you may be sons of your Father in heaven. (Matthew 5:43–45)

>> **key fact** The Sermon on the Mount contains almost all of the important teachings which Jesus gave to his followers.

>> practice questions

1 Why did Jesus say people should use the Lord's Prayer?

2 What did Jesus teach about divorce?

exam tip >>

When you answer a question on the Sermon on the Mount, remember there are many other teachings in the sermon apart from the Beatitudes.

The problem of evil

A Moral evil and natural evil

>> **key fact** People often make a distinction between moral evil and natural evil.

- **Moral evil**: this is evil which is deliberately caused by humans and their actions.
- **Natural evil**: this is the evil, such as earthquakes and natural disasters, which cause harm to people but are not anyone's fault.

Some people say that because there is evil and suffering in the world there cannot be a God or, if there is a God, then that God is not loving. Christians try to find a way of answering these statements.

Why did God not intervene when the twin towers of the World Trade Center in New York were destroyed in 2001? Why did God allow a quarter of a million people to die in the Boxing Day Tsunami of 2004?

Why do animals and babies suffer when it is not their fault and they cannot benefit from the experience in any way?

If God can perform miracles, why does he not help when people are suffering?

'The problem of evil'

Why do some people suffer so much more than others?

Some people say that suffering is a test of faith, but why does God test faith when he knows about a person's faith already?

Why does God create people who are evil? Why does God create people at all if he already knows that they are going to suffer?

B Why does God allow suffering?

- Christianity teaches that God made the world to be perfect. When Adam and Eve ate the forbidden fruit in the Garden of Eden they disobeyed God and brought sin into the world. This is called **the Fall**. From that time everyone has been born with **Original Sin** which damages the relationship between God and humanity. Some people say that because of this, people make wrong choices which lead to natural disasters. This response to 'the problem of evil' comes from the fifth century Christian teacher **St Augustine**.

study hint >>

Many Christians believe that evil cannot be understood and people must simply trust God to do the best for them.

12

- Another way in which Christians try to understand the problem of evil is by saying that God wanted people to have **free will**. Once people have the freedom to choose they must also have the choice of evil as well as good.

- Other people believe that there needs to be evil and suffering in the world otherwise people would not **develop** fully as human beings. For example, people cannot show bravery if there is nothing to be frightened of and people cannot be generous unless there is someone who is in need. Situations such as this help people to develop. This response came from a third century thinker, **St Irenaeus**.

- Sometimes, Christians say that all the evil in the world is caused by **Satan**, the Devil. They believe that it is Satan who encourages people to choose evil rather than good and that he also causes natural disasters and illness. For some Christians, Satan is just a word to describe the opposite to God's goodness and they do not believe he is an actual person. If the Devil does exist it might suggest that God is not all-powerful and cannot control him.

- Finally, some people say that the suffering caused by evil is **a test** from God, to see if people will keep their faith.

C The Book of Job

- In the Bible, there are different approaches to evil and suffering. The book of Job tells the story of **a man who was always faithful to God and followed his teachings. Satan wanted to test Job** and finally God allowed him to. Satan caused Job to lose all his money and animals, his home and, finally, his wife and children. Job still remained faithful to God but wanted to know why he was suffering. God told him that he was far more powerful than Job and that Job did not have the right to challenge him. Once Job realised that he must **accept what was happening** and keep his faith in God **he received back everything that he had lost**, and more.

>> **key fact** There are many other stories in the Bible which show that God does not want people to suffer.

- Christianity teaches that **God will answer prayers** when people ask for help. Jesus, God's son, healed people who were sick and also brought dead people back to life. The difficulty is that although Christians believe that God will answer their prayers they may not always get the response which they were hoping for. In these cases, they have to accept that God knows what he is doing.

>> practice questions

1 Explain some of the different way in which Christians have tried to find an answer to the problem of evil.

2 Explain what the Bible teaches about evil and suffering.

3 'The fact that there is evil in the world proves that God is not all-powerful.' Do you agree with this statement? Give reasons to support your view and show that you have thought about different points of view in your answer.

The church – history

 The Christian Church has developed over nearly 2000 years, since the death of Jesus.

 There are many different divisions and groups in the church.

A Early history

3BCE
Jesus of Nazareth – **Jesus Christ** – was probably born around the year 3BCE in **Bethlehem** in the Roman province of Judaea in what is now Israel. Jesus lived the life of a **Jew**.

30CE
He was **crucified** by the Romans.

After his death and resurrection, he ascended into heaven and his disciples received the **Holy Spirit**. They started to preach **Jesus' teachings**.

35CE
A Jew, **Saul of Tarsus**, was employed to hunt out and persecute these early followers of Jesus. One day, while on the road to Damascus, Saul had a vision that Jesus was calling him. His name was changed to **Paul** and he began to preach the message of Christianity throughout the **Mediterranean**.

250CE
People began to bring together the 27 books of the **New Testament**.

300CE
Persecution of Christians began in the Roman Empire.

392CE
The Roman Emperor Theodosius I made Christianity the **official religion** of the Roman Empire.

591CE
Augustine came to **England** and brought Christianity to the country.

study hint >>

Jesus was a Jew who may not have intended to found a new religion. His early followers were Jews and it was after Paul's conversion that the message of Christianity was preached to both Jews and gentiles (non-Jews).

remember >>

Originally the Christian Church was based in Byzantium and Rome, the two capitals of the Roman Empire.

B Major divisions

1054CE
There was a **split** between the churches in Rome and Byzantium over differences in teaching. These two groups became the **Roman Catholic Church**, based in Rome, with the Pope as its head and the **Orthodox Church**, based in Byzantium, under the Patriarch of Constantinople.

By the fourteenth and fifteenth centuries, some theologians in Europe began to question the power of the Pope and some of the doctrines of the church. In particular, the practice of the 'selling of indulgences' was criticised.

C Conflict

1517	**Martin Luther** nailed a document called the **'95 Theses'** to the door of his church in Wittenberg. These made allegations against the Catholic Church.
1534	Henry VIII made himself head of the church in England. This broke the ties with the Roman Catholic Church and established the **Church of England**.

study hint >>

When answering questions about the church, remember all members of Christian churches are Christians, whatever denomination they belong to.

D Changes

1612	The **Baptist Church** was founded by Thomas Helwys.
1660	George Fox founded the **Religious Society of Friends** (Quakers).
1738	John and Charles Wesley founded the **Methodists**. They split from the Church of England in 1795.
1876	The **United Presbyterian Church** was founded.
1878	William Booth founded the **Salvation Army**.

In the late sixteenth to the early seventeenth century, the **Congregationalist Church** was founded.

>> **key fact** At first, all Christians belonged to one organisation, but over two thousand years they have broken into several thousand different groups, each of which practices Christianity in a slightly different way.

>> practice questions

1 Who was Saul and what happened to him?

2 Explain two reasons why Christians have split into different groups.

Christian denominations

- There are several thousand different denominations in Christianity.

- All these people are Christians who believe in the Trinity and that Jesus was the Son of God.

- The difference between these denominations is found in some of their beliefs and practices.

A Roman Catholic Church

- The **Roman Catholic Church** is based in **Rome** and has the **Pope** as its head. It is believed that the Pope is descended in a direct line from St Peter who founded the church in Rome and, therefore, he has the authority of the **apostles of Jesus**. The Pope is the spiritual leader of the Roman Catholic Church and, together with the Magisterium, is responsible for all the rulings and teachings which it gives.

- As well as their belief in the spiritual authority of the Pope, the Roman Catholic Church believes in the **intercessory power of the saints** and so prayers are said, for example, to the Virgin Mary, asking her to intercede with Jesus.

- The Roman Catholic Church also teaches **transubstantiation**. This means that when the bread and wine are consecrated at the Eucharist, they become the actual body and blood of Jesus.

remember >>

The Roman Catholic Church is the biggest of all the Christian denominations and has members all over the world.

B Protestant churches

>> key fact The Protestant denomination includes many churches such as the Anglican Church (Church of England), Baptists, Methodists and United Reformed Church.

- In 1517, **Martin Luther** was responsible for the beginning of the **Reformation**. He believed much of the Roman Catholic Church was corrupt and was not following God's teachings. The Reformation, which saw the **division** between the **Roman Catholic Church** and **Protestants**, was a split away from Rome.

- The Protestant churches do not recognise the authority of the Pope and instead have their own religious leaders.

C Church of England

- The Church of England came into existence in 1534 when **King Henry VIII** made himself head of the church.

- He had an argument with the Pope because he wanted a divorce from his wife which the Roman Catholic Church would not allow. This broke the ties with the Roman Catholic Church and established the Church of England.

- The spiritual head of the Church of England is the Archbishop of Canterbury, while the temporal head of the Church is the ruling monarch of Great Britain.

remember >>

Christians believe in the Trinity and that Jesus was the Son of God.

D Non-conformist churches

- There are many different non-conformist denominations. These include the Baptists, Methodists, United Reformed Church and the Religious Society of Friends (Quakers). Non-conformists are churches which do not 'conform' or belong to one of the main churches such as the Roman Catholic, Orthodox or Anglican churches.

- Most of these groups do not recognise an overall spiritual leader and some of their communities are completely independent of any organisation.

>> **key fact** All of these groups came into existence because a particular preacher or group of Christians wanted to come together and worship in a particular way.

>> practice questions

1 Why did the Protestants split from the Roman Catholic Church?

2 Why did the Church of England come into existence?

exam tip >>

When you answer questions about Christian denominations, remember to treat all denominations as being equal; they all follow the teachings of Jesus.

Ecumenism

 Ecumenism is the name given to the belief that all churches should try to become more united. It is a movement which encourages Christians to worship together and set aside their differences.

A What issues do Christians disagree about?

1 **The authority of the Pope** – some Christians believe that the Pope is the head of the Church and that Christians should accept his authority. Others disagree.

2 **The ordination of women** – some Christians believe that women should have an equal role with men in Christian ministry. Others believe that men and women have different talents, and that women should not be allowed to bless the bread and wine during the Eucharist (Holy Communion).

3 **The Eucharist** – some Christians believe that when the bread and wine are blessed by the priest, they become the actual body and blood of Jesus. Other Christians believe that they are symbols to remember Jesus' sacrifice on the cross.

study hint >>

It is issues such as the Eucharist, the ordination of women and the authority of the Pope which divide Christians.

>> key fact There are many issues which divide Christians and cause disagreements.

B What is the World Council of Churches?

- The World Council of Churches came into existence in 1948, after the Second World War. Many Christians wanted to do something about restoring peace in the world. These people wanted to **promote ecumenism** by encouraging Christians to work more closely together.

- Many Christians believe it is important to work together, because disagreements and divisions give a bad impression of Christianity's message of love, and prevent Christians from doing important things such as caring for the poor.

- The World Council of Churches was set up to promote **unity**, to act as a **Christian voice** in the world, and to help bring about **peace and justice** in accordance with Christian principles.

- All the main Christian churches, apart from the Roman Catholic Church, belong to the World Council of Churches. They aim to listen to each other and to learn from each other, in the hope that they will grow together rather than apart. They try to emphasise their shared beliefs as Christians, rather than their different ways of worship and different understanding of aspects of Christian teaching.

remember >>

The World Council of Churches was set up in 1948 to help bring peace after the Second World War.

- The WCC holds meetings where members of all different denominations send representatives. They discuss all kinds of issues, such as refugees, the arms race, ecumenism, medical ethics and world debt.

- Christian Aid is the overseas aid agency for the World Council of Churches.

>> **key fact** Ecumenism is the belief that although there are issues which divide Christians, they all share the same belief in Jesus and so should try to unite and work together.

C Other ecumenical groups

- In 1972, the **United Reformed Church** was formed when many Congregationalists and Presbyterians decided that they should join together and become one church rather than different denominations. Many Christians hoped that this would be the beginning of more unity amongst Christians.

- Some ecumenical centres have been established where Christians of all different denominations can worship together, no matter what sort of church they come from.

- **The Taizé community** in France, provides ecumenical worship for thousands of visitors every year. Services are conducted in several languages, and hymns and chants are sung together.

- In the UK, the abbey on the **island of Iona** is used for youth camps and ecumenical worship.

- Both the Taizé community and the abbey on Iona devote much of their time and income to helping the poor in developing countries.

>> practice questions

1 Why do some Christians disagree with each other about the ordination of women?

2 What is an ecumenical centre?

exam tip >>

Remember in your answers that although Christians may belong to different churches they all have the same belief in Jesus and belong to the same religion.

The church – buildings and features

 There are many different types of buildings in which Christians worship, often reflecting the style of worship which takes place inside them.

 Some buildings are very large and elaborate whilst others may be small and plain.

A Anglican and Roman Catholic churches

>> **key fact** These buildings are often built in the shape of a cross, one of the main Christian symbols.

- The head of the cross is usually facing **east**, towards the rising sun.

- The central part of the cross shape is known as the **nave**.

- Many churches have **spires** or **towers**. These are often seen as a sign of reaching up to God.

- All churches have a **font** where babies are brought to be baptised.

>> **key fact** The most important part of all Anglican, Orthodox and Roman Catholic churches is the altar, which is the holy table where the Eucharist is celebrated.

- Many Orthodox churches have onion domes on their roofs instead of spires or towers.

B Non-conformist churches

remember >>

A Baptist church has a pool for baptisms instead of a font.

study hint >>

The most important part of a Roman Catholic or Anglican church is the altar where the Eucharist is celebrated.

- The buildings of the non-conformist denominations, such as those of the Baptist, Methodist and United Reformed churches, are often much plainer than Anglican or Roman Catholic buildings. They are usually called either **churches** or **chapels**.

- These churches will have a table for celebrating the Eucharist but the most important feature is the **pulpit**. It is from here that the Bible is read and sermons are preached. This stresses the importance of the **Ministry of the Word**.

- Most non-conformist buildings have a font, but in a **Baptist** church there is usually a large pool at the front of the building where adults are baptised by total immersion.

- The Religious Society of Friends (Quakers) meet to worship in a **Meeting House**. Quakers have a very simple style of worship where people sit in silence until one of them feels that the Holy Spirit is moving them to speak.

- The buildings in which Christians worship are all designed to be the 'House of God' where Christians can come together and hear the words of God and pray.

C Interior features

- A Quaker Meeting House, usually called a Friends' Meeting House, has a very plain interior and will usually only have chairs and a table. The chairs are arranged so that they face each other. The table is not used as an altar but usually has on it a Bible and a copy of the book, *Quaker Faith and Practice*.

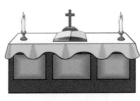

- Non-conformist churches or chapels are usually quite plain. Although there is usually a communion table at the front of the church and there is usually a large pulpit behind and above it. This shows the importance of the 'Ministry of the Word' – readings from the Bible and of the sermon. There may also be a large area for the choir as music plays a very important part in the worship of many non-conformist churches.

- Anglican churches are often more elaborate. At the east end of the church, or sometimes in the very centre of the building, is the **altar** where the Eucharist is celebrated. The **pulpit** for sermons and the **lectern** for the Bible may be either side of this. The **font** is usually placed at the west end of the church by the door.

- Some of the most elaborate churches are Roman Catholic. In a Roman Catholic church there are often several altars, **confessional boxes**, **statues** and many **candles**. There are **stained glass windows** illustrating stories from the Bible or the lives of the saints. On the walls are 14 paintings or carvings representing the **Stations of the Cross** – important events in the last hours leading up to Jesus' crucifixion.

- Orthodox churches are similar in many ways to Roman Catholic churches except that there is an **iconostasis** or **screen** which separates the main part of the church from the altar. The iconostasis is decorated with icons (paintings) of Jesus and the saints and in the centre are the **Royal Doors** which are opened and closed during the services. There are also other icons around the church. Many churches have domes above the iconostasis which help carry sound and also provide another surface for decoration.

>> practice questions

1 What is the most important part of Roman Catholic and Anglican churches?

2 What is a font? What do some churches have instead of a font?

3 Why are many churches built in the shape of a cross?

4 Why do many churches have spires or towers?

exam tip >>

When you are writing about a church building, remember to say which denomination it belongs to and why the different features are important to the members.

Pilgrimage

> 🔖 A pilgrimage is a religious journey. Usually people travel to places they believe have a special holy significance.

> 🔖 Other Christians may believe that a pilgrimage is a journey within themselves.

A Why do Christians go on pilgrimage?

>> key fact A pilgrimage is a religious journey. Some Christians go to special places, while others may say that their whole life is a pilgrimage towards God.

- Unlike some other religions, Christians are not expected or required to go on pilgrimage. It is a matter of **personal choice**.

- Pilgrimages are not holidays. Giving up time to go on pilgrimage might help to **strengthen a Christian's faith** and help them to lead better lives.

- Some Christians set aside time to make the journey because they feel this will help them **get closer to God** in a way that is not possible in their daily lives.

- Others go to special places where they hope they will **receive a cure** for an illness or disease, or to pray for a cure for someone who is not well enough to travel.

B Where do Christians go on pilgrimage?

- In the Middle Ages, pilgrimage was very popular and many people travelled to cathedrals such as **St Albans** and **Canterbury**, to visit relics of the saints.

- Some people also travelled all the way to the **Holy Land** to see the places where Jesus lived, taught and died. Today, many people still travel to the Holy Land to visit Bethlehem, Nazareth and Jerusalem. In Bethlehem, for instance, many Christians visit the Church of the Nativity which stands on the traditional site of the stable where Jesus was said to have been born.

study hint >>

Christians are not required to go on pilgrimages, but they can choose to go, if they want to.

- Another very important place of pilgrimage, especially for Roman Catholics, is **Lourdes** in France. In 1858, a young girl called Bernadette Soubirous had a vision of the Virgin Mary there. A spring of water appeared where the vision had taken place and many people say they have been miraculously cured of illnesses after visiting this place. Many thousands of people go to Lourdes every year and pray for a miracle to heal themselves or others.

- **Santiago de Compostela** in Spain became an important place of pilgrimage in the ninth century. Bones were found there which were believed to be from the body of the apostle James, John the Evangelist's brother. The bones were buried in a tomb under the high altar of the cathedral. 'Santiago' means St James and 'Compostela', field of stars. Pilgrims who visited Compostela wore a badge of a scallop shell which is the symbol of St James.

remember >>

Some people make a pilgrimage in the hope of being cured of something or other people might go on their behalf if they are not well enough to travel.

>> practice questions

1 Give some of the reasons why Christians might go on pilgrimage.

2 What do you think people mean when they say that a pilgrimage is a journey within?

exam tip >>

In your answer, remember that there are different reasons for Christians making a pilgrimage. You should explain what these are.

Prayer

- Prayer is communicating with God.

- Prayer is a very important aspect of life and worship for all Christians.

A What is prayer?

>> **key fact** Prayer is communicating with God. This may be asking God for something or thanking God.

- Prayer is usually made in words, but not always, and can be public or private.

- Sometimes people pray together; this is known as corporate prayer. Sometimes people may pray quietly or silently when they are on their own.

B What types of prayer do Christians use?

- **Petitionary** prayer is when people ask God for something, for themselves or for other people.

- **Intercessory** prayer is when people ask God to intervene in the world at a time of crisis or when people are starving or suffering because of a disaster.

- Many prayers are said to **thank God** for creation and for life and existence in general. Other prayers are to ask God's help in leading a better life.

- Sometimes people use **formal set prayers**, such as those found in the prayer books of the various churches.

- Many Christians pray **spontaneously**, taking an opportunity to speak to God.

study hint >>

There are several different types of prayer: intercessory, petitionary and prayers of thanksgiving.

exam tip >>

When answering questions about prayer, remember that prayers are not just to ask for something, many prayers are said to thank God for creation, for life and for sending his son, Jesus, to earth to save people from sin.

C Prayers

- The **Lord's Prayer**, which Jesus taught at the Sermon on the Mount, is one of the most important and well-known of Christian prayers. You can see the text of the prayer on page 16.

- The **'Jesus Prayer'** is often used in the Orthodox tradition:

    Lord Jesus, Son of God

    Be merciful to me, a sinner.

- The **Hail Mary** is very popular with Roman Catholics:

    Hail Mary, full of grace,

    the Lord is with thee.

    Blessed art thou among women

    and blessed is the fruit of thy

    womb, Jesus.

    Holy Mary, Mother of God,

    pray for us sinners, now,

    and at the hour of our death.

    Amen.

study hint >>

Jesus taught his disciples that when they prayed they should always say the Lord's Prayer.

- Praying is a way in which Christians feel they can **communicate with God**. As well as thanking God and asking for help, prayer makes people feel stronger because they believe they are having a **relationship and conversation with God** who will listen to them.

D ACTS

- Acts is one of the books in the New Testament. Some Christians pray in four parts which they remember as ACTS:

    A: adoration – worshipping God

    C: contrition – acknowledging what they may have done wrong

    T: thanksgiving – thanking God

    S: supplication –– asking God for help.

>> practice questions

1 List four different types of prayer.

2 Why do you think the 'Hail Mary' is a popular prayer for many Christians?

Baptism

- Baptism is the first of the seven sacraments (or religious rites) practised by many Christians.

- When a person is baptised, he or she is either sprinkled with, or totally immersed in water as a sign of purification.

A What is a sacrament?

>> **key fact** A sacrament is a religious ceremony or act regarded as an outward and visible sign of an inward and spiritual grace.

- The seven sacraments are:

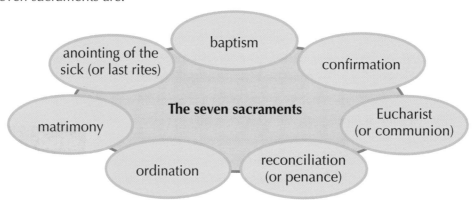

anointing of the sick (or last rites)

baptism

confirmation

The seven sacraments

matrimony

Eucharist (or communion)

ordination

reconciliation (or penance)

- Before the Reformation, the seven sacraments were observed by all Christians. Today, Protestant churches tend to practise only baptism, ordination, the Eucharist and matrimony. However, Orthodox and Catholic churches still observe all seven sacraments.

>> **key fact** Most Christians believe that baptism is a sacrament, an oath or sacred promise to God.

B Why do people need to be baptised?

>> **key fact** Christians believe that because of the disobedience of Adam and Eve in the Garden of Eden all people are born with Original Sin and this needs to be removed before they can begin their lives as Christians.

- Here is a part of the service used during a baptism ceremony:

> Our Lord Jesus Christ has told us
> that to enter the kingdom of heaven
> we must be born again of water and the Spirit,
> and has given us baptism as the sign and seal of this new birth.
> Here we are washed by the Holy Spirit and made clean.
> Here we are clothed with Christ,
> dying to sin that we may live his risen life.
> As children of God, we have a new dignity
> and God calls us to fullness of life. (*Common Worship*)

C What happens at the baptism of a baby?

>> **key fact** In most churches, cleansing of sin takes place when a young baby is baptised.

1. The **baby** is taken to church by its parents.

2. The priest and the family go to the **font** which is usually by the main door of the church.

3. As the baby cannot speak for itself, **godparents** make a promise that they will bring up the child as a Christian.

4. Next, the priest or minister blesses the baby and pours water over its head in the form of a cross, **blessing** it in the name of 'The Father, the Son and the Holy Spirit'.

study hint >>

Most Christians are baptised as babies and godparents make promises on their behalf.

D What happens at the baptism of an adult?

1. Some Christians believe baptism should only take place when a person is able to make the decision for themselves. This is particularly true in the Baptist Church.

2. In the Baptist Church, there is a ceremony of **adult** baptism. In the front of the church is a large tank or pool, covered by flooring. The **pool** is opened and the minister and the person to be baptised stand in it. The person is then baptised by **total immersion**. The minister holds them and they lean back under the water.

>> **key fact** Total immersion is the sort of baptism Jesus is said to have received from John the Baptist.

study hint >>

The most important part of a baptism occurs when water is placed on the person's head and the priest says they are baptised in the name of 'The Father, the Son and the Holy Spirit'.

>> practice questions

1 Why do babies need to be cleansed from sin?

2 What is different about baptism in a Baptist church?

The Eucharist

A What is the Eucharist?

- The word 'Eucharist' comes from the Greek meaning 'thanksgiving'. It remembers Jesus' last meal with his disciples before he was crucified.

>> **key fact** For many Christians, sharing in the Eucharist is the most important part of their worship together because it means they are united as they share the body and blood of Christ.

- In some churches the Eucharist is shared every day, but in others it happens once a week, once a month, or even more rarely.

B How is the Eucharist celebrated?

The celebration of the Eucharist usually follows a pattern:

1. The bread and wine are placed on the altar and the priest or vicar reminds the congregation of what happened at the Last Supper.

2. The **Eucharistic Prayer** is said, **giving thanks to God.**

3. The **bread and wine** are **blessed by the priest** and the words of Jesus at the Last Supper are read.

4. In some churches, the congregation exchange a **sign of peace,** such as a handshake or a kiss.

5. **The bread and wine are shared with the congregation.**

6. The **congregation are blessed** and 'sent out into the world'.

> **remember >>**
>
> The Eucharist service recalls what happened during the last supper Jesus ate with his disciples.

28

C The Eucharistic Prayer

- The celebration of the Eucharist is based upon Jesus' words at the Last Supper:

> The Lord Jesus, on the night he was betrayed, took bread, and when he had given thanks, he broke it and said, 'This is my body, which is for you; do this in remembrance of me'. In the same way, after supper he took the cup, saying, 'This cup is the new covenant in my blood; do this, whenever you drink it, in remembrance of me.' (1 Corinthians 11:23–25)

>> **key fact** Some Christians believe the bread and wine become the actual body and blood of Jesus when they are blessed, in a process called transubstantiation. Others believe they symbolise Jesus' body and blood, but are bread and wine all the time.

- Here is one form of the Eucharistic Prayer:

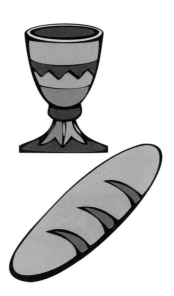

Priest/Minister: Lift up your hearts.

Congregation: We lift them to the Lord.

Priest/Minister: Let us give thanks to the Lord our God.

Congregation: It is right to give thanks and praise.

Priest/Minister: It is indeed right,
it is our duty and our joy,
at all times and in all places
to give you thanks and praise,
holy Father, heavenly King,
almighty and eternal God.
(*Common Worship*)

>> practice questions

1   **What did Jesus say at the Last Supper when he broke bread and drank wine with his followers?**

2   **Give three alternative names for the Eucharist.**

3   **Why is the Eucharist such an important part of Christian worship?**

Confirmation

 Confirmation celebrates the time when people decide for themselves to follow the Christian faith.

 Confirmation is one of the sacraments of the Christian Church.

A What is confirmation?

- If people were baptised as Christians when they were babies, then confirmation gives them the opportunity to confirm for themselves, as adults, that the Christian religion is the one they want to follow.

>> **key fact** Confirmation candidates make for themselves the promises that their parents and godparents made for them at baptism.

> **remember >>**
>
> A sacrament is an outward visible sign of an inward spiritual grace.

- Not all Christian denominations have confirmation ceremonies, because not all denominations have infant baptism. The churches which baptise adults do not feel there is a need for an extra ceremony to confirm promises already made at baptism.

- Most people who are being confirmed prepare for this by going to **confirmation classes**. In these classes, they meet other people who are about to be confirmed, they learn about **what it means to be a Christian** and are taught about the promises they will make, so that they understand what it is they are promising.

B What happens at a confirmation?

>> **key fact** A confirmation service is usually conducted by the Bishop.

 The Bishop asks the confirmation candidates questions and they respond together:

> Do you reject the Devil and all rebellion against God?
>
> *I reject them.*
>
> Do you renounce the deceit and corruption of evil?
>
> *I renounce them.*
>
> Do you repent of the sins that separate us from God and neighbour?
>
> *I repent of them.*
>
> Do you turn to Christ as Saviour?
>
> *I turn to Christ.*
>
> Do you submit to Christ as Lord?
>
> *I submit to Christ.*
>
> Do you come to Christ, the way, the truth and the life?
>
> *I come to Christ.*

2 The Bishop places his hands on the head of each person being confirmed, as a blessing. In some churches, he also puts some oil on their foreheads, as a sign of the Holy Spirit.

3 The Bishop extends his hands towards those to be confirmed and says:

> Almighty and ever-living God,
> you have given these your servants new birth
> in baptism by water and the Spirit,
> and have forgiven them all their sins.
> Let your Holy Spirit rest upon them:
> the Spirit of wisdom and understanding;
> the Spirit of counsel and inward strength;
> the Spirit of knowledge and true godliness;
> and let their delight be in the fear of the Lord. Amen.

4 The Bishop addresses each candidate by name.

> [Name], God has called you by name and made you his own.

5 He then lays his hand on the head of each, saying:

> Confirm, 0 Lord, your servant with your Holy Spirit. Amen.

6 The Bishop invites the congregation to pray for all those on whom hands have been laid.

> Defend, O Lord, these your servants with your heavenly grace,
> that they may continue yours for ever,
> and daily increase in your Holy Spirit more and more
> until they come to your everlasting kingdom. Amen.
> (*Common Worship*)

>> practice questions

1 **Why do people go to confirmation classes before being confirmed?**

2 **Why do some Christian denominations not have confirmation?**

3 **Explain what happens at a confirmation service.**

Funerals

 Christians believe that death is not the end of a person, although it is the end of their life on earth.

 The Bible teaches it is through faith in Jesus and his sacrifice that Christians have the chance of going to heaven.

A What is a funeral for?

- Christian funerals reflect the belief that death is not the end of a person. Although people are sad because a friend, relative or colleague has died, they are encouraged to think about the **promise of resurrection** and **eternal life** made by Jesus. They ask for God's comfort, and thank him for the good qualities the person had, rather than concentrating only on sadness.

>> **key fact** Although a funeral service shows respect for the body of the dead person, it really marks the time when a Christian's soul moves from earth to heaven.

B What happens at a funeral?

- Sometimes, when a person is dying, a priest or minister will come to their bedside to prepare them for death. Prayers will be said and they may receive Holy Communion. If the dying person is a Roman Catholic the priest will anoint them with holy oil. The Roman Catholic and Orthodox Churches believe that this is a sacrament.

- A Christian funeral is usually held a few days after a person has died. This is to allow time for people to be contacted and make arrangements to attend.

- Christianity does not have rules about whether people should be buried or cremated, this is a matter of individual preference.

- A Christian funeral service usually begins with the priest welcoming the coffin into the church and reminding the congregation of the words of Jesus:

> I am the resurrection and the life. He who believes in me will live, even though he dies; and whoever lives and believes in me will never die. (John 11:25b–26a)

This passage stresses the fact that it is through having faith in Jesus and the sacrifice of his own life which he made on the cross that Christians have the chance of going to heaven when they die.

- There are always prayers thanking God for the life of the person who has died, and asking God to comfort the people who remain.

- There are often hymns. The 23rd Psalm – 'The Lord is my Shepherd' – is often read or sung at Christian funerals.

- Someone may then give a short talk remembering the person who has died and the particular qualities he or she had.

- In Roman Catholic churches a special mass (Eucharist) is celebrated at the funeral service.

- In Western societies, friends and relatives often wear dark clothes as a symbol of sadness, but this is a custom rather than a religious rule. Some people prefer to have an atmosphere of celebration for life and wear ordinary clothes rather than special black ones. It is also a custom to send flowers or wreaths to a funeral as a way of paying respect.

- Many people feel the most important aspect of a funeral is that it is an opportunity for people to say goodbye to a loved one, and also to support the family and friends of the person who has died.

- When the coffin or ashes are buried, the priest or vicar reminds people that we came from the ground when Adam was created, and return to the ground at death:

> 'We commit this body to the ground, earth to earth, ashes to ashes, dust to dust.'

study hint >>

At a Roman Catholic funeral a special Requiem Mass is celebrated to thank God for the life of the person who has died and also for the sacrifice of Jesus.

- This also reminds people that the body is unimportant, it is the person's soul that lives on in the afterlife. Christians believe that death is not the end and that people will be resurrected in either a physical or spiritual form and judged by God for the way they have lived.

>> practice questions

1 Why do people wear black clothes at a funeral?

2 What is important about the phrase: 'We commit this body to the ground, earth to earth, ashes to ashes, dust to dust'?

exam tip >>

When writing about funerals, remember they are a sign of respect for the dead person, and also that Christians believe the person's soul has already left their body

Life after death

- Christians believe that when they die they will have the chance of eternal life.

- Many Christians believe they may go to heaven, hell or purgatory, depending on how well they have lived on earth.

A Heaven

>> **key fact** The central Christian belief is that the sacrifice of Jesus on the cross means all people who follow him will have the opportunity of eternal life with God when they die.

study hint >>

Christian teaching does not say what heaven and hell are like but it does suggest hell is an existence where people cannot see God.

- This belief is found in the **Nicene Creed** where it states:

  > We look for the resurrection of the dead, and the life of the world to come.

- It is not clear whether people will go straight to heaven after death, or whether they will wait until the **Day of Judgement**.

>> **key fact** Heaven is viewed as a paradise where people will live with God.

B Hell

- People who have not lived a good life on earth will be sent to hell.

- Christian teaching and opinions about hell have changed over time.

- At one time, hell was believed to be a place of fire and brimstone, where people would be eternally punished by the Devil.

- Today, many people think hell is simply a place where people are forever deprived from seeing God and being happy. In the same way, they see heaven as being eternally in the sight of God.

remember >>

Christians believe that what happens to them when they die depends on how they have lived their lives on earth.

C Purgatory

- Roman Catholics believe there is a place between heaven and hell, called purgatory. Most Catholics are probably not good enough to go straight to heaven because of the sins they have committed on earth, but they have believed in Jesus so they will not go to hell. Instead, they are taken to purgatory where they are punished for a period of time before they are able to enter heaven.

- In 1999, Pope John Paul II described purgatory like this:

> Before we enter into God's Kingdom, every trace of sin within us must be eliminated, every imperfection in our soul corrected. This is exactly what takes place in purgatory.

- He said that purgatory was not a physical place, but a state of being.

D Resurrection

- The Bible is not clear about whether this new life after death is a physical or spiritual one. Some people believe they will be in heaven in their physical bodies, as they were on earth, while others believe it is just their souls which live on for eternity.

- The **Apostles' Creed** says:

> I believe... [in] the resurrection of the body, and the life everlasting.

study hint >>

It is very important to remember that Christians do not believe in reincarnation. They believe that when you die you go to heaven, hell or, perhaps, purgatory. They do not believe that people's souls come back in another being.

>> practice questions

1 **What does the Bible say about life after death?**

2 **Why do you think some people believe in purgatory?**

The Christian year

 The year follows the life of Jesus.

 The year begins at Advent with the four week preparation for the birth of Jesus at Christmas.

A The Christian year

 key fact The Christian year follows the life of Jesus, beginning with Advent.

For Christians, Easter is a more important date than Christmas because this is when Jesus sacrificed his own life to save the people of the world.

1 Following **Advent** is Christmas Day on 25 December.

2 The season of Christmas ends with **Epiphany** on 6 January. This festival remembers the visit of the wise men and the gifts they brought to Jesus. In the Eastern Churches Epiphany also remembers the baptism of Jesus.

3 **Lent** is the 40 days of preparation for Easter.

remember >>

Although some days, such as Christmas, happen on the same date each year, other Christian festivals fall at different times.

remember >>

Advent is the beginning of the Christian year.

4 The Sunday before Easter is **Palm Sunday** when Jesus entered Jerusalem before his crucifixion.

5 The period from Palm Sunday to **Easter Sunday** is **Holy Week**, remembering the last days of Jesus' life on earth.

6 Forty days after Easter is **Ascension Day** which commemorates the moment Jesus ascended into heaven.

7 Ten days later is **Pentecost** (Whitsun), the occasion which marks the coming of the Holy Spirit to the disciples.

8 During the Church's year there are also many **Saints' Days** and other holy days.

9 Some people used to begin the year on March 23rd – **Lady Day** – the day when Mary became pregnant.

>> practice questions

1 What benefits are there in having a yearly cycle of festivals?

2 'Christmas is more important than Easter.' Do you agree? Give reasons to support your view and show that you have thought about different points of view in your answer.

exam tip >>

There are several important days in the Christian year as well as Christmas and Easter and you should mention these in the exam, explaining why they are important.

Advent and Christmas

 Advent is the four week period leading up to Christmas.

 Christmas is the birthday of Christ.

A What is Advent?

- Advent is the four week period leading up to Christmas. It begins on St Andrew's Day, 30th November, or the nearest Sunday to this.

>> **key fact** The word Advent means 'arrival', and Advent is a period of preparation for the celebration of the birth, or incarnation, of Jesus at Christmas.

- Advent marks the beginning of the Church's year.

- Advent is a solemn season, and in the past it was celebrated in the same way as Lent, with fasting and penitence.

- One of the customs associated with Advent is making Advent wreaths. These are rings of evergreens, such as holly and ivy, with four red candles in them. One candle is lit on each Sunday of Advent until all four are burning.

remember >>

The season of Christmas begins with Advent, a time for preparation, and ends with the visit of the Wise Men at Epiphany.

B What is Christmas?

- Christmas is one of the most important festivals of the Christian year.

>> **key fact** Christmas celebrates the incarnation, when God came to earth in human form. No-one actually knows exactly when Jesus was born, and it is more likely to have been in spring than in winter.

- The date of Christmas was fixed by Pope Gregory as late as 354CE. Christmas was placed at this time to absorb the existing pagan festivals of the winter solstice on 21st December. It also incorporated the Roman festival of Saturnalia and the northern European Yule festival.

- The practice of putting models of the manger in churches was started by St Francis of Assisi in the thirteenth century.

C More about Christmas

- The practice of giving presents has two origins. The festival of St Nicholas, the patron saint of children takes place on 6th December, while the visit of the Wise Men to Bethlehem is celebrated by the church on 6th January (Epiphany). Most Christians, however, send cards and give presents at Christmas.

>> **key fact** Advent and Christmas are vitally important because they mark the time when God chose to take the form of a human being and come to earth. This is called the 'incarnation'.

study hint >>

Many of the things we associate with Christmas such as holly and ivy and yule logs are in fact much older, pagan rituals.

>> practice questions

1 Explain what is meant by the incarnation.
2 Why is Christmas celebrated on 25th December?

exam tip >>

When you are writing about Christmas remember the tradition of giving presents really belongs to St Nicholas' Day and to Epiphany.

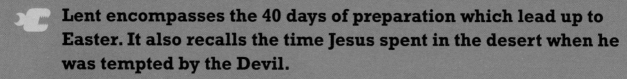

Lent, Holy Week and Easter

> **>C** Lent encompasses the 40 days of preparation which lead up to Easter. It also recalls the time Jesus spent in the desert when he was tempted by the Devil.

> **>C** Easter is considered to be the most important festival in the whole of the Christian year, because it celebrates the resurrection of Jesus from the dead on Easter Sunday.

A Why is Lent important?

>> key fact During Lent, Christians try to make themselves stronger against temptation and prepare themselves for the celebration of Easter.

- **Shrove Tuesday** is the last day before Lent begins. Traditionally people ate pancakes to use up luxury items, such as eggs and butter, before fasting.

- Lent begins with **Ash Wednesday**. Crosses made out of palm leaves for Palm Sunday are burnt and the ashes are used to make the sign of the cross on people's foreheads when they go to church. This shows that they are sorry for the things they have done wrong.

- In the past, Christians used to give up fish and meat entirely during Lent. Today, most Christians do not fast strictly, but many **give up a luxury**, such as alcohol or sweets. This is a reminder of the sacrifice and death of Jesus.

remember >>

Lent is a time of preparation when people try to improve their lives.

B Why is Easter important?

- The week before Easter is **Holy Week** which recalls the last week of Jesus' life.

- The Thursday of Holy Week is called Holy or **Maundy Thursday**. It was on this Thursday evening that, according to the Gospels, Jesus ate the Last Supper with his disciples.

> While they were eating, Jesus took bread, gave thanks and broke it, and gave it to his disciples, saying, 'Take and eat; this is my body.' Then he took the cup, gave thanks and offered it to them, saying, 'Drink from it, all of you. This is my blood of the covenant, which is poured out for many for the forgiveness of sins'. (Matthew 26:26-28)

- The following day is **Good Friday** when, after being tried by both the Jews and the Romans, Jesus was crucified.

- According to the Gospel writers, on the first **Easter Sunday** morning women went to the tomb where Jesus had been buried. The women carried spices in order to anoint Jesus' body. When they got to the tomb, they found the stone across the entrance had been rolled away, and the tomb was empty. They were told that Jesus had been raised from the dead.

study hint >>

Easter proves to Christians that Jesus was the Son of God because he came back from the dead.

>> key fact The resurrection is important, because for Christians it proves Jesus really was the Son of God, and has power over death. Christians believe it shows that they too will have life after death.

C More about Easter

- Easter is not always on the same date every year. It falls on the first Sunday after the first full moon after the spring equinox.

- On Easter Sunday morning, the church bells are rung. The church is decorated with flowers and candles, which were put away during Lent, and the atmosphere of the service is one of celebration. In some countries, there are processions and parades.

- Easter (and other Christian festivals) is celebrated at different times by the Orthodox Church and by the Roman Catholic Church and the Church of England. This is because, in 1582, Pope Gregory XIII introduced the Gregorian Calendar but the Eastern churches did not accept the change and so they continue to use the older Julian Calendar to date religious festivals.

>> **key fact** Easter celebrates the death and resurrection of Jesus, when he overcame the power of death so that people could have eternal life.

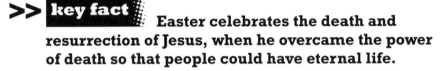

>> practice questions

1 Explain why Easter is so important to Christians.

2 Why do people sometimes give things up for Lent?

exam tip >>

When you are writing about Lent and Easter remember that Lent begins with Ash Wednesday and ends on Holy Saturday. Holy Week is the week before, Easter starting on Palm Sunday when Jesus rode into Jerusalem on a donkey.

Ascension and Pentecost

 Ascension Day is the day Jesus was taken up into heaven.

 Pentecost is the day when the apostles received the Holy Spirit.

A   What is Ascension Day?

- Ascension Day is celebrated on the Thursday which falls 40 days after Easter Sunday.

>> **key fact** Ascension Day commemorates Jesus' ascension, when he was taken up into heaven.

- After Jesus had been raised from the dead, according to the Bible, he met with his disciples and other followers. He ate and talked with them, until he was taken up into heaven. Jesus did not return to earth again.

- On one occasion, while he was eating with them, he gave them this command:

> 'Do not leave Jerusalem, but wait for the gift my Father promised, which you have heard me speak about. For John baptised with water, but in a few days you will be baptised with the Holy Spirit.' So when they met together, they asked him, 'Lord, are you at this time going to restore the kingdom to Israel?' He said to them: 'It is not for you to know the times or dates the Father has set by his own authority. But you will receive power when the Holy Spirit comes on you; and you will be my witnesses in Jerusalem, and in all Judea and Samaria, and to the ends of the earth.' After he said this, he was taken up before their very eyes, and a cloud hid him from their sight.
> (Acts 1:4–9)

- In some churches, special services are held on Ascension Day. In the past, people used to have the day off work so that they could go to church, but today, Ascension Day is often treated as a normal working day rather than a holiday.

study hint >>

Ascension Day was when Jesus finally left his disciples and went to heaven. This was 40 days after Easter.

B   What is Pentecost?

- Pentecost is a Jewish festival called Shavuot which takes place seven weeks after Passover.

>> **key fact**   In Christianity, Pentecost is important because it was at the celebration of this festival that Christians first received the Holy Spirit — according to the Acts of the Apostles — appearing as tongues of flame over them.

remember >>

Pentecost marks the beginning of the Christian Church when the disciples received the Holy Spirit and were then able to heal people and speak in many different languages.

- Pentecost is celebrated on a Sunday seven weeks after Easter.

> When the day of Pentecost came, they were all together in one place. Suddenly a sound like the blowing of a violent wind came from heaven and filled the whole house where they were sitting. They saw what seemed to be tongues of fire that separated and came to rest on each of them. All of them were filled with the Holy Spirit and began to speak in other tongues as the Spirit enabled them.
> Acts 2:1–4

- Pentecost is also known as 'Whitsun' or 'White Sunday' because of the white clothes that many people used to wear.

- Pentecost or Whitsun is known as the birthday of the church, because once the first Christians had the power of the Holy Spirit they were able to spread the message of Christianity.

- Pentecost is traditionally a day for baptisms. In the past, people often dressed in white to represent purity. In some communities, it is a tradition to take part in walks as a demonstration of faith.

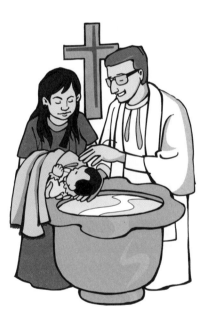

>> **key fact**   Ascension and Pentecost are two very important events because they mark the beginning of the Christian Church.

>> practice questions

1   What does Ascension Day celebrate?

2   On what day of the week is Ascension Day?

3   On what day of the week is Pentecost?

4   Why is Pentecost also known as Whitsun?

5   Why is Pentecost known as the birthday of the Church?

6   In which book of the Bible is the story of how the Holy Spirit was received at Pentecost found?

exam tip   >>

Before his ascension Jesus promised his disciples that the Holy Spirit would come to them and this happened at Pentecost.

Care for the poor

A The prophet Amos

>> **key fact** According to the Bible, caring for the poor is one of the most important ways in which people can show their love for God.

- Amos was an Old Testament prophet who lived in the eighth century BCE.

- The need for social justice was one of the most important aspects of Amos' teaching.

- Amos wrote that God was interested in the way in which the poor were treated not in listening to prayers without action to help the less fortunate.

- He also said that people who did not look after the poor and weak would receive terrible punishments.

B The parable of the sheep and goats

>> **key fact** Jesus often taught in parables which were stories containing a religious message.

- One of the best known of these stories is the parable of the sheep and goats which appears in the Gospel of Matthew, in the New Testament.

- The parable explains that when God judges humanity he will separate people into two groups: the sheep on his right and the goats on his left.

> Then the King will say to those on his right, 'Come, you who are blessed by my Father; take your inheritance, the kingdom prepared for you since the creation of the world. For I was hungry and you gave me something to eat, I was thirsty and you gave me something to drink, I was a stranger and you invited me in, I needed clothes and you clothed me, I was sick and you looked after me, I was in prison and you came to visit me.' ...The King will reply, 'I tell you the truth, whatever you did for one of the least of these brothers of mine, you did for me'. (Matthew 25:34–36, 40)

>> **key fact** Jesus was explaining in the parable that people who cared for others were also caring for him.

C The parable of the rich man and Lazarus

- The parable of the rich man and Lazarus is in Luke's Gospel.
- Lazarus was a beggar who lived in the streets outside of the house of the rich man. When the two men die, Lazarus goes to heaven while the rich man goes to hell. The rich man asks God if he can warn his friends of the consequences if they do not look after the poor but he is not allowed to because they have already been warned by the prophets.

D Agape

- Jesus taught that, by loving their neighbours, people were showing their love for God. When he spoke about neighbours he meant everyone, not just people who lived nearby.
- This type of unconditional and selfless love is called 'agape'.

> 'The most important [commandment],' answered Jesus, 'is this: "Hear, O Israel, the Lord our God, the Lord is one. Love the Lord your God with all your heart and with all your soul and with all your mind and with all your strength". The second is this: "Love your neighbour as yourself". There is no commandment greater than these.'
> (Mark 12:29–31)

exam tip >>

There are many passages from the Bible that can be used in questions about caring for the poor. Try to memorize some of them to put into your answers.

>> practice questions

1 What does the Bible teach about caring for those less fortunate than ourselves?

2 'You cannot be a Christian unless you give time and money to help the poor.' Do you agree with this statement? Give reasons to support your view and show that you have thought about different points of view.

Christian aid organisations

- As a way of putting Jesus' teaching into practice Christians have set up aid organisations to help the poor.

- The best known of these organisations are CAFOD, Christian Aid and Tearfund.

A Aiding the poor

>> **key fact** By supporting aid organisations Christians have the opportunity to put their beliefs about caring for the poor into practise.

- As well as Christian aid organisations, there are many others which are associated with other religions and some, such as OXFAM, which have no religious connections.

- Helping the poor and less fortunate is an important aspect of Christianity. Many Christians support aid organisations or do volunteer work for them as a way of showing their love for God. They follow the example of Jesus who stressed the need to care for the poor.

exam tip >>

Usually, an examination question will ask about a Christian aid organisation and to gain good marks you should write about one which is explicitly Christian.

B CAFOD

- The Roman Catholic Church has an international **overseas development and relief agency** called Caritas. CAFOD is part of this agency and is based in England and Wales.

- CAFOD works with all people regardless of their gender, politics or religion.

- The aim of CAFOD is to **combat poverty and promote justice** in developing countries. It works to enable people to gain access to resources and become self-reliant.

- As well as working with the poor across the world, CAFOD also works to **educate** people, governments and international organisations so that they understand the **real causes of poverty** and work to benefit those who are suffering.

C Christian Aid

Christian ii Aid
We believe in life before death

- The World Council of Churches (WCC) was formed after the Second World War, in 1948, by Christians who wanted to do something about restoring peace in the world. The people wanted to promote ecumenism by encouraging Christians to work more closely together.

- The overseas aid work of the WCC is carried out by Christian Aid.

- Originally it concentrated its work on helping European refugees after the Second World War but it now works in many other countries helping the poor.

- Christian Aid provides **emergency help** at times of disaster and also works on **long term projects**, including literacy and AIDS education.

- The main fund-raising event is Christian Aid Week which is held every May, though other fund-raising activities take place throughout the year.

D Tearfund

- Tearfund is an evangelical Christian aid organisation.

- Like Christian Aid it provides **emergency relief** as well as managing **long-term projects** in the developing world.

- The aim of Tearfund is to help people develop skills so that they do not have to rely on charitable organisations.

TEARFUND
CHRISTIAN ACTION WITH THE WORLD'S POOR

exam tip >>

When you answer questions about these aid organisations you should explain how their work is based on Christian beliefs.

>> practice questions

1 Explain the work of one Christian aid organisation and how it demonstrates Christian beliefs.

2 'If people are poor it is their own fault.' Do you agree with this statement? Give reasons to support your view and show that you have thought about different points of view.

Christian attitudes to money and wealth

 Christianity teaches that being too concerned about money can interfere with their relationship with God.

 Christians believe that rich people should share their wealth with the less fortunate.

A What the Bible teaches about money and wealth

- Jesus taught that rich people should sell their possessions and give their money to the poor so that they would go to heaven when they died.

- Jesus told the poor that they had a special relationship with God:

> Blessed are you who are poor, for yours is the kingdom of God. (Luke 6:20)

- He said that it was not the amount which people gave which was important, but their intent in giving it:

> As he looked up, Jesus saw the rich putting their gifts into the temple treasury. He also saw a poor widow put in two very small copper coins. 'I tell you the truth,' he said, 'this poor widow has put in more than all the others. All these people gave their gifts out of their wealth; but she out of her poverty put in all she had to live on'. (Luke 21:1–4)

- Jesus said that it was not possible to love money and God:

> No one can serve two masters. Either he will hate the one and love the other, or he will be devoted to the one and despise the other. You cannot serve both God and money. (Matthew 6:24)

- He told a rich young man that to gain eternal life in heaven he would have to give away all his riches:

> …'One thing you lack,' he said. 'Go, sell everything you have and give to the poor, and you will have treasure in heaven. Then come, follow me.' At this the man's face fell. He went away sad, because he had great wealth. (Mark 10:21–22)

- Teachings about money and wealth are also found in the Epistles (letters) in the New Testament.

  Paul tells the Christians in Corinth to save money every week so that they are ready to help the community:

> On the first day of every week, each one of you should set aside a sum of money in keeping with his income, saving it up, so that when I come no collections will have to be made. (1 Corinthians 16:2)

  Paul explains to Timothy how dangerous it is to love money:

> For the love of money is a root of all kinds of evil. (1 Timothy 6:10a)

B   Earning money

>> **key fact** Christianity teaches that money should always be earned honestly.

- Most Christians believe that they should work hard and earn money, especially to support their family. However, the work should be honest and earning money should not be the main point of a person's life.

- Christians would not approve of work which exploits other people, such as pornography or gambling, or can harm others, such as selling arms.

- Many Christians feel that they should follow occupations which help others, such as nursing or working for a charity.

C   Wealth and the church

- Many churches are very old and are often very expensive to maintain. This can be costly for the congregation and some people say that these buildings and their furnishings should be sold and the money used for the poor.

- In response, some Christians may say that beautiful buildings for worship are a way of showing respect and love for God.

>> practice questions

1   Explain New Testament teachings about wealth and money.

2   How might Christians show their beliefs about the right use of money in their daily lives?

3   'It does not matter how people earn money as long as they support their family.' Do you agree with this statement? Give reasons to support your view and show that you have thought about different points of view.

The sanctity of life

 Christianity teaches that all people are made in 'the image of God' as it says in the first creation story.

 Because of this Christians believe that human life is sacred.

 Therefore, many Christians believe that life should never be taken away deliberately.

A Christian belief about the sanctity of life

>> **key fact** Most Christians believe that God created people to be special and therefore different from other animals. Many people believe that humans are different from animals because humans have a soul.

> So God created man in his own image, in the image of God he created him; male and female he created them. (Genesis 1:27)

> …the Lord God formed the man from the dust of the ground and breathed into his nostrils the breath of life, and the man became a living being. (Genesis 2:7)

- These passages suggest that human life is different to other forms of life. The phrase 'sanctity of life' is used to mean that all **human life is sacred**.

- Because Christians believe life is sacred they may also think that only God has the right to say when life should end.

> There is a time for everything, and a season for every activity under heaven: a time to be born and a time to die… (Ecclesiastes 3:1–2)

B Made in the image of God

- Being made 'in the image of God' is usually understood to mean that humans share something with God. This is often seen as their **soul**. Christianity teaches that people have a soul which is separate from their body. It is the soul which lives on when a person dies. The soul is intended to go to heaven and live forever.

- Many Christians believe that while humans have a soul, animals do not and this distinguishes humans from other forms of life.

- Most Christians believe that people receive their soul before they are born.

C What this means in practice

>> **key fact** Teachings about the sanctity of life can affect the sort of decisions which Christians make.

- **Abortion:** many Christians believe that a baby is sacred from the moment it is conceived. Because of this they may think that abortion is the same as murder.

- **Euthanasia:** Christians may find it very difficult to accept euthanasia because they believe that only God has the right to end a life.

- **Suicide:** Christians who believe in the sanctity of life might feel that choosing to end their own life would be an insult to God who gave life to them.

- **Capital punishment:** because Christians believe that life is sacred they might not approve of putting someone to death, however serious their crime has been.

- **War:** some Christians, such as the Religious Society of Friends, believe that physical fighting is always wrong, even during a war.

D Other Christian views

- Although Christians believe that life is sacred they may think that, in some circumstances, a life can be ended. They might consider that ending a life is the most loving thing to do in a certain situation. This might happen with a terminally-ill person who is in great pain or when someone knows that a baby is going to be born with no chance of leading a normal life because of an illness or disability.

exam tip >>

Remember not to say that all Christians have the same attitude towards a situation. Although they believe in the sanctity of life they may still have different opinions.

>> practice questions

1 Explain what Christians mean by a soul.

2 Explain how belief in the sanctity of life might affect a Christian's attitude towards euthanasia?

3 'Helping a loved one to end their pain is more important than belief in the sanctity of life.' Do you agree with this statement? Give reasons to support your view and show that you have thought about different points of view in your answer.

Contraception (birth control)

- Contraception (birth control) is the deliberate prevention of pregnancy in a woman.

- Roman Catholics believe that all artificial forms of birth control go against God's plans for humanity. Other Christians may believe that using contraception is sensible because it can prevent unwanted pregnancies.

A — What is contraception?

>> **key fact** Contraception, or birth control, is the deliberate use of natural or artificial means to prevent a pregnancy.

- **Artificial** means of contraception include the Pill, condoms, and 'the coil'. Although these work in different ways, they are all **effective** means of stopping conception.

- Some people also consider the 'morning-after' pill as a form of contraception. However, other people believe that really this is a form of abortion as the egg may have already been fertilised.

- The 'rhythm method' is a **natural** form of contraception. It works by people having sex only at the times of the month when the woman is not likely to be fertile: a much **less effective** form of contraception.

B — Why do people use contraception?

People use contraception for a number of different reasons:

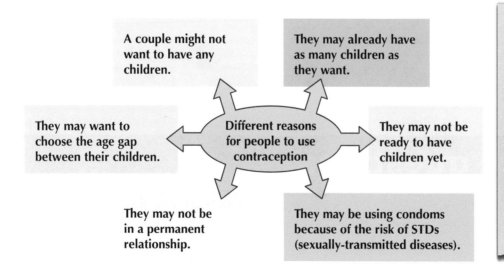

A couple might not want to have any children.

They may already have as many children as they want.

They may want to choose the age gap between their children.

Different reasons for people to use contraception

They may not be ready to have children yet.

They may not be in a permanent relationship.

They may be using condoms because of the risk of STDs (sexually-transmitted diseases).

exam tip >>

When you are answering any question about Christian attitudes towards something, remember to say 'most Christians', 'many Christians' or 'some Christians...'.

C   What do Christians think about contraception?

>> **key fact** Christians often have very different opinions about whether it is right to use contraception. Many believe that if God intended a woman to become pregnant then this should be allowed to happen. Others think that it shows that people are behaving responsibly.

- The **Roman Catholic Church** follows the teachings of 'Natural Law'. The Church considers that conception is a natural outcome of sexual intercourse and therefore believes that anything which is intended to prevent this happening is wrong. The Church says that humans have an obligation to:

  > Be fruitful and increase in number. (Genesis 1:28)

  The Roman Catholic Church believes that sex should also be used for married couples to show their love for each other but that there must always be the chance of pregnancy. Therefore, the Church only permits the use of natural methods of contraception such as the 'Rhythm Method'.

- The **Orthodox Church** does not have a single view about contraception except that the use of the morning-after pill is not permitted. Some Orthodox priests consider that the purpose of sex is for procreation and do not even permit natural methods of contraception. Some priests believe that natural methods are acceptable. Others think that artificial methods are acceptable if used with the blessing of a priest and not simply for selfish reasons.

- The **Anglican Church** ruled that decisions about the number of children people had were a matter for the conscience of the parents and that this would be influenced by God. Therefore, people should decide for themselves.

exam tip >>

Questions in the examination will be about religious attitudes towards contraception, not how different forms of contraception work.

- The **Methodist Church** teaches that contraception is a sensible way of avoiding unwanted pregnancies and that family planning is **responsible Christian behaviour**.

- The **Religious Society of Friends (Quakers)** do not have a collective view on whether contraception is right or wrong. However, many Quakers do use artificial methods of birth control.

>> practice questions

1   Explain two different Christian attitudes towards the use of contraception.

2   'Women have a right to decide whether they have children or not.' Do you agree with this statement? Give reasons to support your view and show that you have thought about different points of view in your answer.

Fertility treatment and embryo research

- Fertility treatment is intended to help people who have problems conceiving a child.

- Embryo research experiments on 'spare' human embryos to develop new medical treatments.

- Some Christians who believe that life begins at conception object to fertility treatment and embryo research.

A   What is fertility treatment?

>> **key fact** Fertility treatment is used by doctors to help women who have been unable to conceive naturally. Some fertility treatment is available on the National Health Service but sometimes people have to pay a great deal of money for it.

What types of fertility treatment are available?

- **AID** is **Artificial Insemination by Donor** where the sperm is donated.

- **AIH** is **Artificial Insemination by Husband**. Usually this is when a man and wife cannot conceive normally and need medical help. Also, some women do not produce fertile eggs and may receive donor eggs from someone else.

- **IVF** is **In Vitro Fertilisation**. Here the egg and sperm are placed in a test tube to form embryos. One or more of these are then transplanted into the woman's womb.

study hint >>

Scientific techniques change and develop very quickly so try to keep up-to-date with the latest news about these.

B   Christian attitudes towards fertility treatment

Many Christians, in particular **Roman Catholics**, do not accept the use of fertility treatment as they believe that it would be **interfering in God's plan**. They believe that if a couple cannot conceive naturally then God did not intend them to be parents.

Others consider that fertility treatment **helps to bring life** into the world and can end the suffering of people who want children but are unable to conceive naturally.

Christians may discuss whether having a baby is a gift from God or a human right.

Even people who believe in the use of fertility treatment may still have **some concerns** about particular aspects of it:

1. During IVF, 'spare' embryos are created and these are generally used for medical research or destroyed. People might consider that each embryo is a human life and should be respected.

2. In AID the sperm comes from a donor who is not the woman's husband and some people see this as a form of adultery.

3. People might think that fertility treatment should not be available to people who are not married, such as homosexual couples, or to people who are too old to conceive naturally. They believe that this is not what God intended.

remember >>

Most Christians believe that life begins at the moment of conception.

C What is embryo research?

- Embryo research uses 'spare' embryos or those gathered from abortions for experiments designed to find new ways of treating many serious conditions, such as Parkinson's Disease or Motor Neurone Disease.

- Sometimes tissue from these embryos can be placed in someone's body to help slow down diseases in the nervous system more effectively than drugs would.

D Christian views on embryo research

- Many Christians accept the use of embryos in research. In the case of an embryo from an abortion they may feel that although the termination of the pregnancy was not welcomed some good has come from it. They see the **healings performed by Jesus** and his teachings about love and compassion as supporting this.

- Other Christians object to the research, as the embryo cannot give consent to its use and is **not regarded as a valuable human life**.

>> practice questions

1 Explain why different groups of Christians might disagree about the use of fertility treatment.

2 'If embryo research helps to stop suffering then it must be the right thing to do.' Do you agree with this statement? Give reasons to support your view and show that you have thought about different points of view in your answer.

Abortion

A What is meant by 'abortion'?

- When a pregnancy ends naturally and a woman has a miscarriage this is called a **natural abortion**. However, what most people mean when they use the word abortion is a **procured abortion** when the woman makes a decision to have a medical procedure which will end the life of the embryo or foetus.

- Most Christians are opposed to abortion because they believe that God intends the birth of each human life and that to prevent this is really **murder**. Others would disagree with this view and say that in some circumstances an abortion might be the **kindest action to take**, perhaps because the baby would be born with such a serious illness that it will be unable to live normally or because having the baby would seriously harm the mother.

B What are the reasons for having an abortion?

- The woman might be at risk of seriously damaging her physical or mental health if she has the baby.

- A woman might be pregnant because she has been raped and does not feel she could accept the baby.

- There could be strong medical evidence to suggest that the baby would be born with very serious health problems.

- The woman may feel that her circumstances are not suitable for bringing up a child: she might be too young; she might already have children and the family could not cope with another baby; she might be single; or she might feel that having a baby at a particular time would affect her career.

> **study hint >>**
>
> The Bible does not say anything directly about abortion and Christians have to apply other relevant teachings when deciding their views about it.

C The law and abortion

- In order for a woman to be given an abortion in the United Kingdom, two doctors have to agree that the procedure is being carried out for a good reason.

- In the United Kingdom, abortion has been legal since 1967. Most abortions are carried out as soon as possible, but they can be performed up to the 24th week of the pregnancy. After this the foetus would be considered to be **'viable'** which means it could probably survive outside of the womb without medical support.

D God's plan

> Before I formed you in the womb I knew you, before you were born I set you apart. (Jeremiah 1:5)

- Together with other passages from the Bible this teaches that God has planned the life of each individual. For many Christians this means that from the moment of conception, or even before, God intends for that individual to be born.

E Christian points of view

- The teaching of the **Roman Catholic Church** is that abortion is wrong. The only circumstance in which an abortion may take place is when it is known that the baby will die but that it is essential to operate on the woman. An example of this is in the case of an ectopic pregnancy. An operation is necessary to save the woman's life and the baby would die anyway. This teaching is called the **Doctrine of Double Effect**.

- The **Anglican Church** believes that abortion should not be chosen unless it is the **last resort**. However, it teaches that abortion is the best alternative in some circumstances and that the decision must be left to the people involved.

- Some other churches share the Anglican view that abortion may be a last resort but it is never to be welcomed. They may believe that it can be the kindest action to take, particularly if the mother is too young or the baby is likely to have serious health problems.

exam tip >>

In your answers to questions about abortion remember to give different Christian views.

>> practice questions

1 Explain why Christians might disagree about abortion.

2 Explain the Christian teachings which people might use when talking about abortion.

3 'Abortion is legalised murder.' Do you agree with this statement? Give reasons to support your view and show that you have thought about different points of view in your answer.

Euthanasia

 In the UK, it is against the law for someone to take any action which can hasten another person's death. This applies even if the person is in enormous pain and has already asked someone to help them to die.

 Most Christians would disagree with euthanasia.

A Types of euthanasia

- Euthanasia is formed from two Greek words, 'eu' and 'thanatos' which mean a good death. Euthanasia, therefore, is often called 'a good or easy death'.

Active euthanasia: when action is taken to end someone's life by giving them a lethal injection for example.

Passive euthanasia: this is when treatment is stopped which is all that is keeping a person alive.

Ways of classifying euthanasia

Involuntary euthanasia: when other people decide that a patient should die. This could happen if the patient is in PVS (Persistent Vegetative State).

Voluntary euthanasia: when a person asks to be given help to die, and makes it clear that this is his or her own choice.

B Church teaching on euthanasia

- The Roman Catholic Church teaches that euthanasia is wrong. However, it does not require life to be maintained by extraordinary means (such as being on a life-support machine) and in these circumstances a patient can be allowed to die naturally.

- Other Christians also agree that it is unnecessary and perhaps cruel to use drugs and machines to keep people alive if it is known that they have no hope of recovery.

C Why some Christians support euthanasia

- Christians may say that, in some situations, helping a person end their pain by dying is the most loving thing to do. The Bible teaches to 'do to others what you would have them do to you' (Matthew 7:12). Therefore, if you would like to be allowed to die rather than end your life in great pain, you should allow this for other people.

- Christians might say that because God has given people free choice they should be allowed to make their own decisions about when is the right time for them to die.

- Some Christians might say that to keep patients alive on drugs when they are very ill is, in fact, interfering with God's plan for them to die.

D Why some Christians are opposed to euthanasia

- Many Christians are opposed to any form of euthanasia. They believe that life is a gift from God and that only God has the right to decide when to end a life.

- Some Christians believe that suffering can bring them close to God. They may say that being in great pain can help them to understand what Jesus suffered when he died for the sins of humanity on the cross.

- Another argument which some Christians make is that if euthanasia was made legal relatives might encourage elderly members of their family to die in order to save on hospital bills and the cost of care homes.

- Many Christians believe that rather than euthanasia, people should be given the chance to end their life with dignity and should go into a hospice for their last days.

> **remember >>**
>
> **There is no specific teaching about euthanasia in the Bible.**

>> practice questions

1 Explain why Christians might have different views about euthanasia.

2 How might Christians use the teachings of the Bible and the church when they are discussing euthanasia?

3 'Only God has the right to end a life.' Do you agree with this statement? Give reasons to support your view and show that you have thought about different points of view in your answer.

The hospice movement

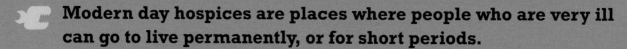

> **⊂** Modern day hospices are places where people who are very ill can go to live permanently, or for short periods.

> **⊂** Hospices aim to help people to live out the end of their lives with dignity and without pain.

A The hospice movement

>> **key fact** Many Christians believe that instead of euthanasia there are better ways in which a person can be helped to have a dignified death. Hospices are specialist nursing homes where people are looked after by trained and experienced medical staff.

- The **first hospices** were founded by the Crusaders in the eleventh century, as places where the **incurably ill were admitted** for care.

- The modern hospice movement in the UK was founded by **Dame Cicely Saunders** (1918–2005). She was a doctor who became particularly concerned about a Polish patient whom she had met. He was dying in pain without family or friends for comfort. On his death he left her money to build a hospice. Cicely Saunders set up the first UK hospice, **St Christopher's**, in 1967.

- There are now hospices all across the world, many caring especially for children.

B What is the purpose of a hospice?

- Hospices are designed to provide care for terminally ill people.

- They provide opportunities for these people and their carers to take a break from home care.

- Hospices provide specialised medical pain-killing treatments.

- As well as providing counselling and support for patients they also work to help their families. They may continue to support and comfort the families after the patient's death.

>> **key fact** Many, but not all hospices are run by Christians.

C Christianity and the hospice movement

- Hospices welcome all people, not just Christians. Hospice staff are not required to be Christians.

- It is not part of the responsibility of hospice staff to convert patients to Christianity but there are often religious services and visits from ministers and priests for people who want religious support.

- Many Christians have devoted their lives to working in and for the hospice movement. Because of their faith they believe that everyone should have the right to live and die with dignity. Christians believe that people are made in the 'image of God' and that they should treat those who are dying as they themselves would want to be treated.

- Many people see hospices as a better choice than euthanasia because people there have the opportunity to say goodbye to their families and end their life in as much comfort as possible.

study hint >>

Many Christians support the work of hospices because of their belief that all human life is sacred.

D Blessed Mother Teresa and hospices

- **Blessed Mother Teresa of Calcutta** (1910–1997) was a nun who, through her Christian faith, believed people should be allowed to die with dignity. Mother Teresa worked with the poorest people in India and saw many dying at the roadside with no medical care. She began to set up hospices in India and provided care which showed **her belief that every human life was of importance to God**

- Blessed Mother Teresa **opened the first home for the dying in 1952**, on land given by the City of Calcutta. She converted an abandoned Hindu temple into the Kalighat Home for the Dying, which is a free hospice for the poor. The name Kalighat means the 'Home of the Pure Heart'. Poor people were given **medical attention and the chance to die with dignity according to the way of their faith**. This meant that Muslims were read to from the Qu'ran, Hindus were given water from the sacred River Ganges and Catholics received Holy Unction. A second hospice, Shanti Nagar (City of Peace) was set up for leprosy sufferers.

>> practice questions

1 Where did the hospice movement begin?

2 Explain the aims of modern hospices.

3 Explain why a Christian might support the work of a hospice.

War

 Christians have different opinions about fighting in a time of war.

 In the Bible, there are passages where God commands war and other places where Christians are told to love their enemies. Therefore, Biblical teaching can be used to support the arguments for or against war.

A Biblical teaching used to support fighting in a war

- The Bible says that people should defend the weak and oppose evil.

- There are many examples in the Old Testament where God commands people to go to war.

  Proclaim this among the nations: Prepare for war! (Joel 3:9)

- This has been used to suggest that sometimes God wants people to fight physically against their enemies.

- In the New Testament there is one occasion when Jesus uses physical force. He overturns the tables and benches of the money-lenders and the dove-sellers in the Temple in Jerusalem. He considered that they were misusing the Temple which was for the worship of God (Mark 11:15).

- Some Christians might say that this shows that Jesus thought it was sometimes acceptable to use violence.

- Jesus did have some contact with soldiers (e.g. Luke 7:1–10), but the Gospels do not suggest that he thought they were wrong to have this job.

- Many Christians believe that it is right for people to fight for their country in wartime. They would say that otherwise evil might overcome good.

- For some Christians fighting in a war might be seen as an example of love, to risk their lives to protect others.

  Greater love has no one than this, that he lay down his life for his friends. (John 15:13)

B Just War

A war can be described as 'Just' if it is fought according to certain conditions.

These conditions were first drawn up by Thomas Aquinas (c.1225–1274). They were then developed by Francisco de Vitoria (c.1492–1546).

The conditions of a Just War are:

 The war must be declared by a proper authority such as a government.

 There must be a good reason for going to war, which does not include greed.

 The intention of the war must be to do good and stop evil. Therefore, wars cannot be fought out of revenge in order to intimidate people.

 War must only be fought as a last resort after all other ways of solving the problem have failed.

The war must do more good than it causes harm.

 The war must be possible to win, otherwise lives are being risked for no purpose.

 The people involved in the fighting should not use any more violence than is strictly necessary.

These conditions were designed to prevent war whenever possible and also to limit its bad effects.

C What the Bible says about war and violence

There are several places in the New Testament where Jesus teaches his followers the value of peace.

In the Beatitudes Jesus clearly advocates making peace:

> Blessed are the peacemakers, for they will be called sons of God. (Matthew 5:9)

Further on in the Sermon on the Mount he says that it is not enough to love people who love you but that his followers should:

> Love your enemies and pray for those who persecute you. (Matthew 5:44)

Finally, during Jesus' arrest in the Garden of Gethsemane, when the High Priest's servant goes to arrest Jesus, one of the disciples draws his sword and cuts off the servant's ear:

> 'Put your sword back in its place,' Jesus said to him, 'for all who draw the sword will die by the sword'. (Matthew 26:52)

study hint >>

There are often different ways of interpreting the Bible and some people use different texts from the Bible to argue different things.

>> practice questions

1 Explain some of the Biblical teachings which might be used in a discussion about war.

2 What are the conditions of a Just War?

3 'Christians must be pacifists.' Do you agree with this statement? Give reasons to support your view and show that you have thought about different points of view in your answer.

Human rights

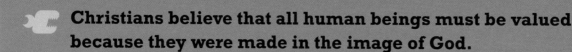 Christians believe that all human beings must be valued because they were made in the image of God.

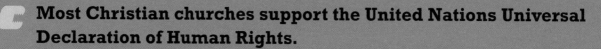 Most Christian churches support the United Nations Universal Declaration of Human Rights.

A The Universal Declaration of Human Rights

- In 1948, the General Assembly of the United Nations signed the Universal Declaration of Human Rights which declared the **rights of all human beings**. This declaration followed the events of the Second World War (1939–1945).

- The Declaration states that all **people must be treated equally and without discrimination**, that everyone has the right to a **fair trial**, that **no-one should be tortured**, that **people should not be imprisoned without good reason** and that people must be **free to hold any opinions** which they choose.

- Teachings in the Bible support the values outlined in the Declaration:

> For I was hungry and you gave me something to eat, I was thirsty and you gave me something to drink, I was a stranger and you invited me in, I needed clothes and you clothed me, I was sick and you looked after me, I was in prison and you came to visit me. (Matthew 25:35–36)

B Liberation theology

- Liberation theology is a movement within the Roman Catholic Church which began in South America in the 1960s.

- In some of these countries, such as El Salvador, the majority of people were very poor while friends of the government were very rich. When people protested about the government they were usually arrested and either imprisoned without trial or they simply 'disappeared'.

- Liberation theology maintains that Christians cannot allow these things to happen without trying to stop them. It teaches that it is part of the duty of a Christian to **fight against injustice, poverty and oppression** wherever it is found.

- Father Camillo Torres and Archbishop Óscar Romero were two South American Catholic priests who were assassinated because they supported Liberation theology.

- Some Christians, including the Pope, consider that Liberation theology is too political. They believe that Christians should not take direct action in this way but should work and pray for peace.

C Amnesty International

amnesty international

- Some Christians actively campaign for human rights by working with organisations such as Amnesty International.

- Amnesty International was founded in **1961** by a British lawyer, **Peter Beneson**.

Amnesty International's vision is of a world in which every person enjoys all of the human rights enshrined in the Universal Declaration of Human Rights and other international human rights instruments. In pursuit of this vision, Amnesty International's mission is to undertake research and action focused on preventing and ending grave abuses of these rights.

>> 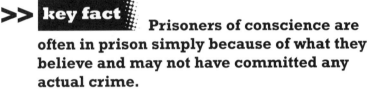 **key fact** **Prisoners of conscience are often in prison simply because of what they believe and may not have committed any actual crime.**

- Amnesty International **protests** directly to governments who they believe are abusing human rights and runs **letter-writing campaigns** to demand fair treatment.

- Amnesty International has **over two million members** in more than 150 countries.

study hint >>

Amnesty International is non-religious. However, many Christians support it because they believe that its work reflects Christian principles that all human beings must be valued because they are made in the image of God.

>> practice questions

1   Explain Christian teachings which might be used in a discussion about human rights.

2   Why might Christians support the work of organisations that campaign for human rights, such as Amnesty International?

Capital punishment

 Capital punishment is often called the death penalty. It is when someone is put to death for their crimes.

 While many Christians are opposed to capital punishment, some believe that it is supported by the Bible.

A Aims of punishment

>> **key fact** Christianity says that God is all-loving and will always forgive. Jesus taught that Christians should love and forgive everyone, even their enemies. However, this does not mean criminals should not be punished for breaking the law.

- People say there are four main reasons to punish criminals:

  Deterrence – to set an example so that other people do not commit the same crime

  Protection – to protect society from criminals

  Reformation – to make criminals realise what they have done is wrong and to help them become better people

  Retribution – to punish criminals by making them pay for their crime.

- Sometimes Christians might decide to try to **work with criminals** in order to persuade them to stop their criminal activities.

B Christian arguments in support of capital punishment

- The Ten Commandments say that **murder is wrong but some Christians might still approve of capital punishment**.

- The Bible says that there are some crimes for which people should be put to death:

  > Anyone who strikes a man and kills him shall surely be put to death.... Anyone who attacks his father or his mother must be put to death. (Exodus 21:12, 15)

- According to the Bible the weak must be protected. The death penalty means that a criminal cannot repeat a crime and is used in order to protect people from criminals.

- Some Christians think that the death penalty might be more humane than making a person spend the rest of their life in prison.

- The death penalty shows that justice has been carried out and might make other people think before they commit the same crime.

>> **key fact** The UK stopped using capital punishment in 1965, but since then some people have tried to bring it back for very serious crimes.

C Christian arguments against capital punishment

- Jesus said that people should forgive each other:

  > Then Peter came to Jesus and asked, 'Lord, how many times shall I forgive my brother when he sins against me? Up to seven times?' Jesus answered, 'I tell you, not seven times, but seventy-seven times'. (Matthew 18:21–22)

- In order to carry out the death penalty someone has to be the executioner. This could be damaging for the person who has to do the job.

- The prisoner has no chance of reforming their life.

- There have been occasions where it has been discovered that a person was innocent only after they have been executed.

- Jesus taught that people should not judge one another:

  > Do not judge, or you too will be judged. For in the same way you judge others, you will be judged, and with the measure you use, it will be measured to you. (Matthew 7:1–2)

D What the churches say about capital punishment

- The Roman Catholic Church has not totally condemned the use of capital punishment, though it teaches that in most cases there are better ways of punishing criminals.

- The Church of England is totally opposed to the reintroduction of capital punishment. It teaches that people should be punished for their crimes but that the justice system must be merciful.

- The Religious Society of Friends is totally opposed to capital punishment:

  > …judicial execution serve(s) no purpose… (and) …brutalises the society that kills. (The Quaker Statement on the Death Penalty)

>> practice questions

1 Describe Christian teachings about capital punishment.

2 'People who kill deserve to be killed themselves.' Do you agree with this statement? Give reasons to support your view and show that you have thought about different points of view in your answer.

Pacifism

- Pacifism teaches that it is never right to use violence.

- Pacifists will not fight during a war, even in defence of their own country.

- Pacifists believe that any protest must only use peaceful means.

A What is pacifism?

>> **key fact** Pacifism is the belief that violence, war and taking peoples' lives are unacceptable ways of resolving disputes.

- Pacifists understand that there will always be occasions when there are conflicts and disputes. However, they believe that these should be met with **non-violent protests**. They will take part in demonstrations, boycotts and non-cooperation but without any use of violence.

- People who refuse to fight during a war are known as 'conscientious objectors'. However, even though they will not fight, these people may still be in the front line of fighting: driving ambulances and caring for people in other ways.

- Pacifism and non-violent protest is not just limited to times of war. In the twentieth century, **Gandhi** protested against British rule in India with *satyagraha*, a Hindu practice of non-violent protest. Later, in the 1960s, **Martin Luther King Jr.** led peaceful protests against racism in the USA. His followers took part in sit-ins, boycotts, marches and demonstrations but all without violence.

B The Religious Society of Friends (Quakers)

- The Quakers are a Christian denomination which has always been opposed to the use of violence.

> We utterly deny all outward wars and strife, and fightings with outward weapons, for any end, or under any pretence whatever; this is our testimony to the whole world. The Spirit of Christ by which we are guided is not changeable, so as once to command us from a thing as evil, and again to move unto it; and we certainly know, and testify to the world, that the Spirit of Christ, which leads us into all truth, will never move us to fight and war against any man with outward weapons, neither for the kingdom of Christ, nor for the kingdoms of this world. (Quaker Declaration of Pacifism to Charles II, 1660)

remember >>

Many Christians are pacifists, but not all.

- Quakers 'fight' using the **'weapons of the spirit'**: love, truth and co-operation.

C Why are some Christians pacifists?

- Christians believe that all human life is sacred because it was created by God who made people 'in his image'. Therefore, many believe that they should not use violence against other people.
- Some Christians believe that the sixth commandment 'you shall not murder' (Exodus 20:13) means that all killing is wrong.

Jesus said:

> Blessed are the peacemakers, for they will be called sons of God. (Matthew 5:9)

He also said:

> If someone strikes you on the right cheek, turn to him the other also... But I tell you: Love your enemies and pray for those who persecute you... (Matthew 5:39b, 43)

- Many Christians who are pacifists base their beliefs on Jesus' teaching about love:

> A new command I give you: Love one another. As I have loved you, so you must love one another. (John 13:34)

>> practice questions

1 **Explain why some Christians might fight in a war whilst others will not.**

2 **'All Christians must be pacifists.' Do you agree with this statement? Give reasons to support your view and show that you have thought about different points of view in your answer.**

Prejudice

- Prejudice is a pre-formed opinion, usually an unfavourable one, about a person or thing.

- Most prejudice is usually based on ignorance and lack of knowledge.

- When people put their prejudices into action this is called discrimination.

>> **key fact** There has been prejudice and discrimination throughout history. Many of the cruelest events in history, such as slavery and the Holocaust, have been caused by prejudice.

A Prejudice and the law

- People may be discriminated against for many reasons: **age, disability, gender, physical appearance, race, religion, skin colour or sexuality**.

- In 1948, the Universal Declaration of Human Rights stated that:

> Everyone is entitled to all the rights and freedoms set forth in this Declaration, without distinction of any kind, such as race, colour, sex, language, religion, political or other opinion, national or social origin, property, birth or other status.

- In the United Kingdom, the Sex Discrimination Act of 1975, the Race Relations Act of 1976 and the Disability Discrimination Act of 1995 made many forms of discrimination illegal. However, people continue to discriminate against those who are in some way different from themselves.

B What the Bible says about equality

- The Old Testament says that all people must be treated with respect and cared for. It is also clear about the treatment of strangers.

> When an alien lives with you in your land, do not mistreat him. The alien living with you must be treated as one of your native-born. Love him as yourself, for you were aliens in Egypt. I am the Lord your God. (Leviticus 19:33–34)

- In the New Testament, Paul wrote that Christianity removes barriers between people.

> There is neither Jew nor Greek, slave nor free, male nor female, for you are all one in Christ Jesus. (Galatians 3:28)

C The parable of the Good Samaritan

- Jesus told a parable about a traveller who was robbed, mugged and left at the roadside. The two Jews who passed by ignored the injured man. Then, a Samaritan (a man of a different race usually discriminated against by the Jews) stopped and helped the man. Jesus asked:

> 'Which of these three do you think was a neighbour to the man who fell into the hands of robbers?' The expert in the law replied, 'The one who had mercy on him'. Jesus told him, 'Go and do likewise'. (Luke 10:36–37)

D Christianity and racism

- Racism can take many forms. One example of racism in history is the apartheid system in South Africa. Before 1990, South Africa had a system of laws which were called apartheid. This meant that black and white people were separated. Black people lived in poverty with no political rights. Protests were usually dealt with violently.

- Christianity teaches that **all people are equal in the sight of God** and should be treated equally.

- For many centuries Christianity had a poor record in relation to equal rights. For example, many slave owners were Christians.

- However, there are Christians who have devoted their lives to fighting injustice in the world. People such as Martin Luther King Jr., **Archbishop Trevor Huddleston** and **Archbishop Desmond Tutu** are just some of the many Christians who have spent their lives fighting racism.

remember >>
There is nothing in the New Testament which supports racism.

>> practice questions

1 **Explain the Biblical teachings which might be used in a discussion about racism.**

2 **How might Christians put their beliefs about racial equality into practice in their daily lives?**

The fight against racism

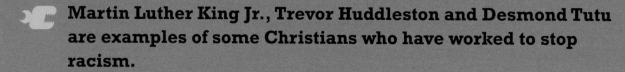

- Martin Luther King Jr., Trevor Huddleston and Desmond Tutu are examples of some Christians who have worked to stop racism.

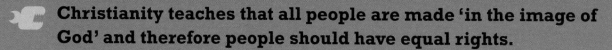

- Christianity teaches that all people are made 'in the image of God' and therefore people should have equal rights.

A Martin Luther King Jr. (1929–1968)

- Martin Luther King Jr. was a black American minister. He lived in America at a time when it was within the law to discriminate between black and white people. For example, black people had to sit on different train carriages to white people.

- He was a pacifist, who believed that the use of violence showed hatred not the love of God. Therefore, he organised **peaceful non-violent protests** against these laws.

- Martin Luther King Jr. campaigned against issues, such as separate restaurants, separate schools and separate seats on buses for black and white people. He led **marches and protests against injustice**.

- His most famous speech was delivered on the March to Washington in 1963:

> I have a dream that my four little children will one day live in a nation where they will not be judged by the color of their skin but by the content of their character...And when this happens, when we allow freedom to ring, when we let it ring from every village and every hamlet, from every state and every city, we will be able to speed up that day when *all* of God's children, black men and white men, Jews and Gentiles, Protestants and Catholics, will be able to join hands and sing in the words of the old Negro spiritual: *Free at last! Free at last! Thank God Almighty, we are free at last!*

- In 1964, Dr King was awarded the Nobel Peace Prize. However, in April 1968, he was shot dead but James Earl Rae.

exam tip >>

In an examination answer about people who have worked against racism or other forms of discrimination you must mention how their Christian beliefs influenced them.

B Archbishop Trevor Huddleston (1913–1998)

- Trevor Huddleston was an Anglican priest and a member of the Community of the Resurrection. He spent many years of his life working in South Africa opposing apartheid.

- He believed that Christians have a **duty to prevent people being treated unfairly** and that it would be **un-Christian to do nothing** in these circumstances.

- In 1981, he became President of the Anti-Apartheid Movement.

- He persuaded many people to **boycott all South African goods** and **not to play sports against South African teams**. He argued that to deal normally with South Africa would be to support apartheid.

- Trevor Huddleston was friends with many black leaders such as Oliver Tambo, the President of the African National Congress, and Archbishop Desmond Tutu.

- Although Trevor Huddleston died in 1998 he saw the results of his work, with the abolition of apartheid in 1994.

C Archbishop Desmond Tutu (1931–)

- Desmond Tutu was the first black South African Anglican Archbishop of Cape Town. In 1984, he was awarded the Nobel Peace Prize for his work in opposing apartheid. In 2005, he was awarded the Gandhi Peace Prize. Like Martin Luther King Jr. and Trevor Huddleston he believes it is his **Christian duty to oppose any abuse of human rights by non-violent protest**.

>> practice questions

1 **Explain how and why one well-known Christian has worked to fight racism.**

2 **'All Christians must fight against racism.' Do you agree with this statement? Give reasons to support your view and show that you have thought about different points of view in your answer.**

Family

- Christian marriage services emphasis that, except for the elderly, one of the principle reasons for marriage is for a couple to have children and bring them up as Christians.

- Christianity teaches that the family has a central role in religious life.

A The role of the Christian family

- Christianity teaches that family members have duties towards one another:

Family members should support each other through difficult times as well as celebrating special events.

It is a duty of a Christian family to bring up the next generation to follow the Christian faith.

Families have a responsibility towards their members who are sick or elderly.

Families should provide children with their first experiences of love and forgiveness.

- Many Christians give their time to support organisations which help strengthen family life.

B What the Bible says about the family

- The fifth commandment says:

> Honour your father and your mother, so that you may live long in the land the Lord your God is giving you. (Exodus 20:12)

- The Bible also teaches that families must care for each other:

> If anyone does not provide for his relatives, and especially for his immediate family, he has denied the faith and is worse than an unbeliever. (1 Timothy 5:8)

> Children, obey your parents in everything, for this pleases the Lord. Fathers, do not embitter your children, or they will become discouraged. (Colossians 3: 20–21)

C The Mothers' Union

The Mothers' Union is a Christian organisation with more than 3.6 million members in over 78 countries worldwide. It campaigns for families across the world. Despite its name, men can also become members.

The Mothers' Union also provides practical help for families such as:

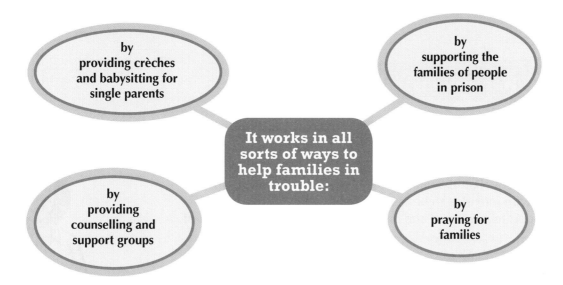

Family life has changed since the time when the Bible was written. Two thousand years ago the majority of people may have lived in extended families. In the twenty-first century an increasing number of people live together without being married and also many children are brought up in single-parent families.

The Christian Church accepts that this is a reality and works in particular to support single parents bringing up children alone. However, Christianity still teaches that God's design is for a man and a woman to be married and to have children.

Most Christian churches do not accept same-sex couples, and so do not welcome the idea of same-sex couples bringing up children.

>> practice questions

1 Describe Biblical teaching about the importance of the family.

2 'It is the duty of Christian parents to make their children follow the Christian faith.' Do you agree with this statement? Give reasons to support your view and show that you have thought about different points of view in your answer.

3 Explain why Christians might support the work of an organisation such as the Mother's Union.

Gender

 Different groups of Christians may disagree about the roles of men and women, both in the family and in the church.

 The Church of England took many years to decide to ordain women priests and still cannot agree whether it should be possible for women to become bishops.

A Women in Christian society

- At the time of Jesus, the society in the Holy Land was mostly dominated by men. Some Christians believe that this should still be the case.

- They think that men and women have **different strengths**. Men are intended to be leaders and a woman's role is to support her husband and care for their family. The Bible says:

> Wives, submit to your husbands as to the Lord. For the husband is the head of the wife as Christ is the head of the church, his body, of which he is the Saviour. Now as the church submits to Christ, so also wives should submit to their husbands in everything.
> (Ephesians 5:22–24)

- Others think that, in the modern world, men and women **should be treated equally**. Both men and women should be able to go out to work and they should share childcare and work in the home.

> You are all sons of God through faith in Christ Jesus, for all of you who were baptized into Christ have clothed yourselves with Christ. There is neither Jew nor Greek, slave nor free, male nor female, for you are all one in Christ Jesus. If you belong to Christ, then you are Abraham's seed, and heirs according to the promise.
> (Galatians 3:26–29)

INTERNATIONAL WOMEN'S DAY

study hint >>

Although there are many places in the Bible which seem to suggest that women should be secondary to men, it was completed almost 2000 years ago and some Christians think that these teachings are now out-of-date.

B Women in the church

Neither the Roman Catholic nor Orthodox Churches allow women to be ordained as priests.

- This is because they believe that when a priest celebrates the Eucharist he is representing Jesus and a woman cannot do this.

- Also, according to the New Testament, Jesus chose only men to be his apostles.

- The Bible also says that women should not preach or speak in church.

Other Christian denominations such as the Methodist Church and the United Reformed Church do have women ministers. Since 1994, the Church of England has ordained women as priests.

- These denominations believe that the teaching of equality is very important and that women can lead a church community as well as a man.

- They also argue that, in some ways, the New Testament reflects the society of the time it was written but that it would be wrong to continue to discriminate against women today.

>> practice questions

1 What Biblical teachings might be used in a discussion about equality between men and women?

2 'Christians should always treat men and women equally.' Do you agree with this statement? Give reasons to support your view and show that you have thought about different points of view in your answer.

3 Explain why Christians disagree about the ordination of women.

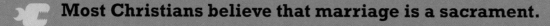

Marriage and divorce

- Most Christians believe that marriage is a sacrament.

- Christians who are married should always treat each other with love and respect.

- None of the Christian churches encourage divorce and people should remain married until they are separated by death.

A Christian teaching about marriage

>> **key fact** Although many people choose to live together without being married. Christians believe that marriage is a special relationship which is blessed by God.

- The Bible teaches that from the time when Adam and Eve, the first humans, were created, God intended them to live together.

> For this reason a man will leave his father and mother and be united to his wife, and they will become one flesh. (Genesis 2:24)

- Most Christians believe that marriage is a sacrament – the outward physical sign of an inward invisible grace – which cannot be broken.

B A Christian wedding ceremony

1. A Christian couple may decide to talk to a priest or minister before they are married.

2. In the service they make vows to each other: that they will love each other, be faithful to each other and stay together until they die. These views are made in public and 'in the presence of God'.

3. The couple then usually exchange rings to symbolise their relationship.

4. Prayers are said for the couple, including a prayer for Gold to bless them with children.

5. In the Roman Catholic Church there is then a special Nuptial Mass.

C What the Church teaches about divorce

- No Christian welcomes divorce because of the teaching in the Sermon on the Mount where Jesus says:

  > But I tell you that anyone who divorces his wife, except for marital unfaithfulness, causes her to become an adulteress, and anyone who marries the divorced woman commits adultery. (Matthew 5:32)

- However, all of the Christian Churches recognise that sometimes marriages break down. In these circumstances they accept that divorce may be inevitable. In many of them, including the **Church of England**, these divorced people are usually **allowed to remarry in church** because of Jesus' teaching of love and forgiveness.

- The **Roman Catholic Church is particularly strict about remarriage**. If a couple separate but are not divorced they are still welcomed into the Church. However, if they obtain a divorce the Church will not remarry them. Sometimes it is possible for a couple to obtain an annulment from the Pope. This is a document which states that because of particular circumstances (such as one half of the couple having been too immature to understand the significance of the marriage service) the marriage did not in fact take place. The couple are then free to remarry someone else in a church ceremony.

D Relate

- Relate is a secular organisation which works to help people who have problems in their relationships by providing them with **counselling**.

- Many Christians support the work of organisations such as Relate because it can help to keep relationships together.

>> practice questions

1   'People should not expect a marriage to last for the rest of their life.'
    Do you agree with this statement? Give reasons to support your view and
    show that you have thought about different points of view in your answer.

2   Explain Christian teachings about the importance of marriage.

3   Explain why Christians have different views about divorce.

The environment

- The Bible teaches that God created the world and that all life belongs to God.

- Christians believe that they have a role as stewards and must take care of the planet.

- Because of environmental damage many plants and species are threatened.

A   The environment

>> **key fact** Scientists have shown that the earth is facing serious problems for the future because of the damage caused by humans.

Deforestation – rainforests are cut down for timber or farming. This contributes to climate change and threatens the life of animals that live in the forests.

Depletion of resources – things such as coal and oil are being used up. There is only a finite amount of these so there may be nothing left for future generations.

Global warming — the overall temperature of the earth is increasing and this is said to be causing changes to the climate, such as the melting of the polar ice caps.

Pollution – caused by emissions from factories and petrol vehicles as well as the unsafe disposal of waste materials.

- Some Christians believe that humans are superior to all other life forms and are therefore responsible for the problems facing the world's environment.

B   Christian stewardship

- The Bible says that God made the world at the beginning of time. God put humans in charge of the world and instructed them to be stewards of the earth. Stewards look after things for someone else, therefore Christians believe that they have a **responsibility to take care of the environment for God**.

> So God created man in his own image, in the image of God he created him; male and female he created them. God blessed them and said to them, 'Be fruitful and increase in number; fill the earth and subdue it. Rule over the fish of the sea and the birds of the air and over every living creature that moves on the ground.' (Genesis 1:27–28)

C What might Christians do to help care for the planet?

1. They could try to **waste less** food and fuel.

2. They could try to use **'greener' types of energy**.

3. They could **recycle** as much of their waste as possible.

4. They could try **alternative ways of travelling** such as walking or cycling.

5. They could **support candidates for local and national government** who promise to help the environment.

6. They could **support organisations** such as Greenpeace or the Worldwide Fund for Nature.

7. Most importantly, as Christians, they could **pray** for the future of the planet.

remember >>

Christians believe that they have a particular duty to tackle the problems facing the environment.

>> practice questions

1. Explain why Christians might believe that they have a duty to care for the world.

2. Explain why some Christians might support the work of an environmental organisation.

3. 'God made the world so God should take care of it.' Do you agree with this statement? Give reasons to support your view and show that you have thought about different points of view in your answer.

Science and religion

- Some people believe that because scientific theories show that the universe probably started with a massive explosion, the creation stories in the Bible cannot be true.

- Some Christians believe that the Bible is true and that therefore scientists must be wrong.

- Other people think scientists and the Bible could both be right, but in different ways.

A Scientific theories v. biblical teachings

>> **key fact** Most scientists believe the universe started with a huge explosion, known as the 'Big Bang'.

- The Bible teaches that **God made the world in six days**. On the seventh day he rested. It also says that God made everything which was on the earth and was pleased with it.

  > God saw all that he had made, and it was very good. (Genesis 1:31a)

- The Bible teaches that God made humans at the time of creation. It says that these first people were Adam and Eve and that all humanity is descended from them.

- Most scientists do not believe that people existed on the earth at the beginning but that they evolved over millions of years. This came about through a process known as **natural selection**. Weaker animals which were not able to adapt to their habitat died out and only the stronger ones survived. This idea was first brought to the public's attention by **Charles Darwin** who wrote *On the Origin of Species by Means of Natural Selection or the Preservation of Favoured Races in the Struggle for Life*, in 1859.

- In the book of Genesis there are two quite different accounts of the Creation. In Genesis 1:1–2:2, God created the world in six days and restedon the seventh.

  Day 1 – light and darkness

  Day 2 – earth and sky

  Day 3 – water, land and plants

  Day 4 – sun and moon

  Day 5 – sea creatures and birds

  Day 6 – animals and humans

  In Genesis 2:3–3:24, God makes the earth and then a human being. He makes the Garden of Eden for the human to live in and then he makes all the other animals.

B Creationism

Creationist Christians believe that the world was created exactly as described in the book of Genesis.

Creationists argue that the Bible is the revealed 'Word of God' and therefore everything in it is true exactly as it is written. In the book of Genesis there is an account of how God made the world and so this must be how the world was made. Some people have even suggested that so-called scientific evidence, such as fossils, was placed there by God to confuse people who do not accept the truth of the Bible.

C The biblical story of creation: truth or myth?

Some Christians do believe that the Genesis accounts of creation are true, others think that these stories are myths.

- Some people say that the stories of creation in Genesis are myths. This means that they are not literally true but may contain important ideas. These people may believe that God did make the universe and all life in it. However, they do not believe that these stories are literally true or that God made the earth in six days.

- Other Christians argue that it is wrong to suggest that some parts of the Bible are true while others are not. They also argue that because the Bible is the revealed word of God, everyone must accept that it is true.

>> practice questions

1 'If Christianity is right, then science is wrong.' Do you agree with this statement? Give reasons to support your view and show that you have thought about different points of view in your answer.

2 Explain why some Christians might think that parts of the Bible are mythical.

Religion and the media

 Christians sometimes use the media in order to spread the message of Christianity.

Many Christians are concerned about the influence the media can have on society.

A How might Christians use the media?

- **Posters** and advertisements might be used to inform people about Christianity and local Christian events.

Easter Sunday Service 8 pm

- Church **newspapers** can inform people about events in their local Christian community.

Church Today

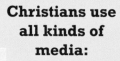

Christians use all kinds of media:

- The **Internet** is often used to teach people about religious beliefs.

- Both **television and radio** can help people learn about Christianity or share in worship in their own homes.

B Why might Christians be concerned about the media?

- Advertising might **make people unhappy** because they want what other people have but they cannot afford it. It might also encourage them to spend money on luxuries rather than using it to help the poor.

- Films and television can often give **the impression that crime and violence are normal activities**. Some Christians may feel that the portrayal of sex and the use of drugs in the media might encourage younger people to experiment in these areas.

- Some newspaper journalism causes much unhappiness by **unnecessarily exposing the details of people's private lives**.

- The Internet might also **lead more people into looking at pornography or gambling** which many Christians believe to be wrong.

remember >>

Most Christians do not think that the media is a bad thing but they may be concerned about some of the ways in which it is used.

Christians and censorship

- Many Christians believe that there should be stricter controls on what is published. They think there is too much sex and violence in the media and that this encourages people to live un-Christian lives by following these examples.

- However, other Christians believe that adults should be allowed to make their own choices about what use they make of the media. Other people should not interfere.

>> practice questions

1   Why do some Christians think that the media has advantages, as well as disadvantages?

2   'Christians should not allow their children to watch television.' Do you agree with this statement? Give reasons to support your view and show that you have thought about different points of view in your answer.

Exam questions and model answers

These model answers provide an outline of how you could construct your response. Space does not allow us to give a full response. The examiner will be looking for more detail in your actual exam responses.

Central beliefs

A **Explain what happened at the crucifixion of Jesus.**

Christians believe on Good Friday, after his trial, Jesus was taken to be crucified as he had predicted. As was the normal practice, he was nailed to a cross by his hands and feet and left to die. The cross was placed between two criminals. He was given vinegar in a sponge to drink by a Roman soldier. After three hours, he prayed to God, and then he died. A Roman soldier then pushed a spear into Jesus' side to make sure that he was dead. Blood and water ran out. His mother Mary and John the disciple were with him when he died.

> *This is a straightforward answer which gives a clear account of the crucifixion containing all the important information. In a question like this, there is no need to go beyond the actual events of the crucifixion. The opening sentence helps to put the answer into context.*

B **Explain what happened immediately after Jesus' death.**

A rich man called Joseph of Arimathea asked the Roman authorities for Jesus' body. The body was taken down from the cross and placed in a newly-made tomb which belonged to Joseph. A stone was rolled over the entrance to the tomb to cover it. Because it was almost time for the Jewish Sabbath to begin, the body was then left until Sunday.

> *The question asks for an 'explanation' of what happened 'immediately' after Jesus' death. The answer explains what happened and why, e.g. 'because it was almost time for the Jewish Sabbath'. There is no need to go beyond this to the resurrection.*

C **'It is impossible for Christians in the twenty-first century to follow the example of Jesus.' Do you agree? Give reasons to support your answer and show you have thought about different points of view.**

Some people might think that it is impossible to follow the example of Jesus because of all the pressures they are under in modern life. They may feel that they have to work so hard to support their family that they do not have the time to pray and go to church or even to think about helping other people.

Many Christians would argue that following the example of Jesus is the most important thing that a Christian can do and that following his example and caring for other people should take priority over everything else. They might feel that although it would be almost impossible to follow his example, nevertheless they should try.

I am not a Christian but I think that if people believe in Jesus then they should do everything they can to follow his example because they believe that he is the Son of God.

> *This is a good response taking two viewpoints and supporting them well, as well as giving a personal supported view.*

D **Explain how and why Christians might show respect for the Bible in their daily lives.**

The Bible is not treated in the same way as the holy books of some other religions but it is shown respect by Christians. The Bible is believed to be the revealed 'Word of God' and is, therefore, very important. Christians will keep a Bible clean and safe and not treat it like any other book. Some Christians read the Bible every day so that they can learn more about God's teachings. In a church, there is often a very large Bible from which people read during the service. In some churches, this is shown great respect and is carried in a procession before it is read. Some people may stand when readings are taken from the Gospels. Other Christians show their respect for the Bible simply by trying to follow its teachings in their daily lives.

> *This is a good answer. It explains the importance of the Bible as well as showing how this importance may be reflected in the way the Bible and its teachings are used.*

E **'Christians should pay more attention to the New Testament than to the Old Testament.' Do you agree? Give reasons to support your answer and show you have thought about different points of view.**

The whole Bible is important to Christians and is believed to be the revealed word of God, so it is a guide to what God wants and how people should lead their lives. The Old Testament is the Bible of the Jews and shows how God led the Jews to be a chosen people and how they learnt from God's teachings.

Some Christians may feel that the New Testament is more important because it contains the accounts of Jesus' life, his teachings and the teachings of the early church. It also contains details about the work of the Holy Spirit in the Christian Church.

I believe that, as the whole Bible is regarded as the revealed 'Word of God', both parts are equally important. Jesus was a Jew and would have been very familiar with the writings in the Old Testament and it is important for Christians to understand these as well.

> *The answer accepts that the New Testament may be seen as more important because it contains the teachings of Jesus, but also acknowledges a different view about the importance of the Old Testament.*

History and Christian life

A **Explain why the three main Christian groups are the Roman Catholic, Orthodox and Protestant churches.**

At first, the Christian Church was based in Rome and Byzantium (Constantinople). In 1054CE there was a split between the churches in Rome and Byzantium over differences in teaching. These two groups became the Roman Catholic Church based in Rome with the Pope as its head and the Orthodox Church based in Byzantium under the Patriarch of Constantinople. In the foutenth and fifteenth centuries, some theologians in Europe began to question the power of the Pope and some of the doctrines of the church, in particular the selling of indulgences which were believed to shorten the time people spent in purgatory. In 1517, Martin Luther nailed a document called the '95 Theses' to the door of his church in Wittenberg. These made allegations against the Catholic Church. This led to the formation of the Protestant churches who were protesting against the Roman Catholic Church.

> *In a question like this, with limited time to answer, it is important to get the key facts down on paper. This answer picks the main points for the three denominations and expresses them clearly.*

B   **'Each Christian group should be proud of the teachings and practices which make it special and different.' Do you agree? Give reasons to support your answer and show that you have thought about different points of view.**

Each of the Christian churches is different. They all have particular practices which are important to them. The Orthodox Church is one of the oldest and is very proud of its traditions and the way in which it worships. The Roman Catholic Church is the largest Christian group. However, although people think that their particular practices and beliefs are very important, they are all Christians who follow the example of the life and teachings of Jesus and they all believe that Jesus was the Son of God who gave his life to save humanity from sin. Therefore, some people believe that the churches should forget their differences and come together in one group.

Although I agree with the statement in principle, I do believe that God intended for everyone to come together in worship and not to be split up in this way. Personally I think that the different denominations should set aside their differences and come together as one church.

> *This is a good response which clearly shows two sides to the discussion and has a well-supported personal view.*

C   **Explain the importance of the main features of a Christian place of worship.**

The buildings used by Christians for worship are often quite different from each other. However, many have the same main features although their importance may vary. The font is one of the most important features because it is where babies are baptised and welcomed into the Christian church. The font is usually found near the main door of the church. The altar is also very important. It usually stands towards the east end of the church, though sometimes it is right in the centre. The Eucharist is celebrated on the altar. Another very important feature is the pulpit. This is a raised platform where the priest or minister may stand to give the sermon. It is placed high up so that everyone can hear. Sometimes the pulpit is also used for Bible readings. In some churches, the Bible is read from a special stand called a lectern which shows its importance.

> *The question asks for the 'main' features. The answer focuses on four features which are all important with regard to Christian faith and worship. The opening sentence shows that the candidate is aware that not all churches and their features are the same.*

D   **Explain one example of ecumenism in Christianity.**

One example of ecumenism is the World Council of Churches. This was founded after the Second World War, in 1948, by Christians who wanted to do something about restoring peace in the world. Many Christians believe it is important to work together, because disagreements and divisions give a bad impression of the Christian message of love and prevent important aims, such as caring for the poor. The World Council of Churches was set up to promote Christian unity, to act as a voice in the world, and to help bring about peace and justice in accordance with Christian principles. Christian Aid is the overseas aid agency for the World Council of Churches.

> *There are many examples which could have been chosen here, such as the work of an ecumenical centre or community, but the World Council of Churches is a good example and the answer explains its purpose clearly.*

Sacraments

A   **Explain the meaning and importance of baptism for Christians.**

Baptism is a sacrament – the outward visible sign of an inward invisible grace. It is important for Christians because the baby is blessed and is now free from Original Sin. It has become a member of the Christian Church. Some other Christians, such as Baptists, believe that baptism should wait until the person is old enough to make the decision for themselves. In the Baptist Church, people choose to be baptised as adults and this takes place by total immersion in a large pool at the front of the church.

> *The question asks for an explanation and the answer provides a good account of the purpose of baptism, in cleansing Original Sin, as well as the welcoming of the baby into the Christian Church. It also explains different baptism practices.*

B   **Explain what is said and done at an infant baptism.**

At an infant baptism the baby is brought to church by its parents. The priest, the parents and the godparents stand by the font. The priest holds the baby and asks the godparents to make promises on its behalf. They promise that they renounce the devil and will bring the baby up to be a Christian. The priest then makes the sign off the cross with water on the baby's forehead and blesses the baby in the 'Name of the Father, the Son and the Holy Spirit'. Sometimes each person at the ceremony carries a candle because Jesus brought light into the world. The baby is now cleansed of Original Sin and has been welcomed into the Church as a member of the Christian family.

> *The question does not ask for a baptism in any particular denomination and the answer is therefore a general description of the ceremony. All the main details are included, in particular the use of the Triune name: 'Father, Son and Holy Spirit.'*

C   **Explain what is said and done at a Christian funeral.**

At a Christian funeral the body is usually taken into a church in a coffin. It is placed at the front of the church while a priest or minister conducts a short service. Someone will say something about the life of the person who has died. Prayers are said asking God to take care of the person in the hope that they have now gone to heaven. The person leading the service reminds the congregation that Jesus said, 'I am the resurrection and the life'. After the service, the body may be taken to a graveyard to be buried or to a crematorium to be cremated. The words, 'ashes to ashes, dust to dust' are said to remind people that their bodies return to the earth but their souls go to heaven.

> *This is a good account of a typical Christian funeral containing all the important details and explanation. The quotation is useful because it shows an understanding of this particularly Christian teaching about death.*

D   **Explain how beliefs about the afterlife might affect the way Christians live.**

Christians believe if they follow the example of Jesus and his teachings and accept him as the Son of God they will go to heaven when they die. They may also believe if they do not do this they will go to hell. Therefore, they may make sure throughout their life that they always try to act in the way Jesus taught, in particular they may follow his teaching of 'agape' or Christian love.

> *The answer shows the essential Christian beliefs about life after death. It would also have been possible to mention purgatory here. It shows that Christians must believe in Jesus as well as follow his teachings.*

A   **'Easter is the most important Christian festival.' Do you agree? Give reasons to support your answer and show you have thought about different points of view.**

Easter recalls the time when Jesus overcame death. On the Sunday morning, when the women visited the tomb they found that it was empty and Jesus was alive again. This means that all followers of Jesus now had the opportunity to receive eternal life and need not fear death. Because of this, Easter is the most important Christian festival. Most people would agree that Christmas and Easter are the two most important festivals. However, some people believe that Christmas is particularly important because this was the moment when God chose to become man and live on earth as Jesus. This is called the Incarnation.

My own opinion is that although I enjoy Christmas more, Easter remembers Jesus' sacrifice for humanity by giving up his life, so Easter has to be the most important festival.

> *The answer is well-balanced, it shows two points of view about the statement as well as a personal view and each is well-supported with argument.*

Wealth and poverty

A   **Explain why Christians might give money to charity.**

The Bible teaches that people should give money to charity and Christians should try to follow these teachings. Many Christians give money to church collections at Sunday services so that the church can continue to help less fortunate people. Some Christians give as much as a tenth of their income to the church to help the poor. This is called tithing. In the early church in Jerusalem, the deacons collected charity to help the widows. Jesus taught several parables about charity. These include the widow who gave almost all she had to the poor and also the rich man whom Jesus told to sell all his possessions. Christians who give money in this way are following Jesus' teaching.

> *This is a good answer. It shows different ways in which Christians might give to charity as well as explaining this with reference to the Bible.*

B   **Explain why Christian might support the work of a Christian organisation which helps the poor in developing countries.**

Christians are taught in the Bible that they have a duty to help the poor. There are teachings in the Old Testament such as in book of Amos as well as Jesus' parables and the Sermon on the Mount in the New Testament.

Jesus taught the 'Golden Rule': to treat others as you would wish to be treated. Christians recognise that they should always try to help those who are less fortunate. One of the ways in which Christians can do this is by supporting the work of an organisation such as Christian Aid.

Christian Aid helps everyone it can, whether they are Christian or not and, as well as helping in emergencies, it also undertakes long-term projects so that eventually these people can take care of themselves.

> *This is a good answer. The candidate has given several reasons about why a Christian would support the work of a Christian aid organisation and has explained them. Although the question did not ask for the name of an organisation, the reference to Christian Aid is helpful.*

C **'People should look after their own family before they worry about the poor.' Do you agree? Give reasons to support your answer and show you have thought about different points of view.**

Everyone must have a duty to look after their family first. Many Christians would say that their family has to be their first responsibility and they must look after them before they can worry about other people. In several places in the Bible the responsibility of parents and children is made very clear.

However, Christians do believe that they have an obligation to look after the poor especially when there is so much poverty, disease and suffering in the world. Jesus told his disciples not to be concerned with their own wellbeing. He also asked them to put the needs of others first. The parable of the sheep and the goats shows that God will judge people by how they helped others who were in need.

Personally, I think that Christians have to try to strike a balance between these two positions. Of course they have to look after their family but once that is done then caring for the poor should come before spending money on luxuries.

> *This is a good answer: different supported views are given and the candidate has given their own supported response.*

Medical ethics

A **Explain Christian teachings that might be used in a discussion about abortion.**

The Bible does not say anything directly about abortion. Many Christians believe that the instruction not to commit murder in the Ten Commandments applies to abortion.

Christians disagree about when the foetus becomes a human being and therefore when an abortion could take place. Many Christians, in particular Roman Catholics, believe that the embryo receives its soul and becomes a person at the moment of conception. This means that any abortion would be murder. The Roman Catholic Church only permits abortion when it is a known but unintentional side-effect of a treatment needed to save the mother's life, this is called 'Double Effect'.

There are other Christians who believe that the foetus does not become a human being until much later in its development and therefore think that in certain circumstances, perhaps when the pregnancy is the result of rape, abortion may be the most loving choice.

> *This is a good answer. The candidate has shown good understanding of teachings about abortion and also explained why Christians might have different opinions about this.*

B **Explain how a Christian might try to help someone who is considering suicide.**

Christians believe that suicide is wrong. They believe that life is a gift from God and that life is sacred because God said 'Let us make man in our image, in our likeness' (Genesis 1:26). Also, the Ten Commandments tell people not to commit murder and some people may think that suicide is like murdering themselves. However, Christians realise that people would only want to commit suicide when they are so unhappy that they feel they have no other choice. Therefore, most Christians, while trying to persuade someone not to kill themselves, would offer them help and support, perhaps also recommending that they contact an organisation like the Samaritans.

> *This is a good answer. The candidate has shown that they understand the arguments about suicide and can also explain how a Christian might try to help.*

C **'Every woman has the right to have a baby.' Do you agree? Give reasons to support your answer and show you have thought about different points of view. You must refer to Christianity in your answer.**

Some Christians might say that because women are designed by God to have babies this statement is true. However, many Christians would say that a baby is a gift, not a right. Therefore, the woman must accept that it is God's will that she should not have a child.

Many Christians object to fertility treatment. They believe that the way in which the sperm is collected is against the Bible's teachings and also that it is wrong to discard or experiment on the unused embryos as they have the right to life. They would also say that interfering with conception in this way goes against natural law. Others believe that God has enabled doctors to develop fertility treatment and so they use this to help women who cannot conceive naturally.

I am not sure of my own opinion about this as I do not really think that a baby is a right but on the other hand if I was desperate to have a baby and fertility treatment was the only way then I would probably want to try it.

> *This is a good answer. The candidate has structured and balanced the different views and has given a personal supported opinion.*

War, peace and justice

A **Explain Christian attitudes towards war.**

Many Christians are pacifists and believe that all war is wrong. They base this on the fact that they believe that Jesus was a pacifist. However, some Christians believe that there are occasions, such as a Just War, when fighting may be necessary. A Just War has to meet certain conditions, such as it is necessary to ensure civilians are not harmed in the action. Some Christians would point out that there are examples in the Bible of God ordering wars to be fought. There are some Christian groups which are committed to pacifism under all circumstances. The best know of these is the Religious Society of Friends (Quakers). They believe that any physical violence is wrong and that there are always other ways of dealing with a situation.

> *This is a good answer. The candidate has explained clearly a variety of different Christian attitudes towards war.*

B **Explain why Christians might work to help people who are victims of human rights abuse.**

Christians believe that everyone was created in the image of God. Because of this they believe that everyone has the right to be treated equally. Throughout the Bible, in both the Old and New Testaments, there are teachings which show how people should be treated. Jesus said that the second most important commandment was to treat your neighbour as yourself.

Although the Universal Declaration of Human Rights was signed in 1948 there are many places in the world where people do not have the rights to which they are entitled.

Many Christians choose to support or work for organisations, such as Amnesty International, which run letter-writing campaigns to protest against individual cases of human rights abuse.

Others believe that Jesus' teachings require direct action in fighting for the poor and oppressed and following the teachings of liberation theology, often at the risk of losing their own lives.

> *This is a good answer because the candidate has explained why Christians might want to help, as well as giving good examples of practical assistance.*

C **'All Christians must be pacifists.' Do you agree? Give reasons to support your answer, and show you have thought about different points of view. You must refer to Christianity in your answer.**

Some Christians say that all people must be pacifists because they believe that Jesus was a pacifist and never hurt anybody, although this is not quite the same. Some Christians believe that the commandment 'do not commit murder' means that any fighting must be wrong because someone might be killed. Jesus told people that they should 'turn the other cheek' and not to seek revenge. This seems to suggest that even in self-defence fighting is wrong.

Other Christians believe that in certain circumstances, such as a 'Just War', it is necessary for Christians to fight, not to fight would let evil win and so be a sin itself.

I find it difficult to know whether there are any circumstances when it would be right to fight. During the Second World War it was necessary to fight to prevent the Nazis dominating the world. I know that I could not stand by and do nothing if my family were being attacked. It would be wonderful if everyone was a pacifist but they are not and therefore there will always be occasions when everyone, including Christians, may have to fight.

> *This is a good answer because it is balanced and different points of view have been considered and explained. The candidate has also explored their own response to the statement.*

Family, relationships and gender

A **Explain how a Christian marriage ceremony might reflect religious beliefs.**

There are different ways in which a Christian wedding ceremony may reflect religious beliefs.

Traditionally, the bride wears a white dress as a symbol of purity and virginity. The ceremony is usually held in a church with the couple standing in front of the altar. During the service they make vows to each other that they will stay together until one of them dies and that they will be faithful to each other. These vows are important because they are made in front of God as well as before the congregation. This means that if they break one of these vows they are breaking a promise to God. Usually the couple exchange rings. The rings symbolise unity: the unity of the couple being married and also the unity of God's love.

During the service the priest or minister reminds the couple that one of the purposes of marriage is for the couple to have children and bring them up as Christians.

For most Christians, marriage is seen as a sacrament which is something which cannot be undone.

> *This is a good answer. It explains in detail how the marriage ceremony can reflect belief and does not waste time on descriptions of what happens which would gain very few marks.*

B   **'Divorce is always wrong.' Do you agree? Give reasons to support your answer and show you have thought about different points of view. You must refer to Christianity in your answer.**

Many Christians would say that, for Christians, divorce is always wrong because in the wedding ceremony they promised to stay together until 'death do us part'. Some Christians might also say that if people do get divorced, they are breaking a promise they made to God as well as to each other. This means that Christians cannot take divorce lightly.

On the other hand, some Christians may believe that people should consider a divorce if they have tried everything else and living together is making them very unhappy. Christians will always try to help people whose marriages are in trouble but this does not always work. Jesus said that divorce was only allowed in cases of adultery, however he also taught love and forgiveness and some Christians might say that it is not always possible for a couple to get over their problems and stay together.

My personal opinion is that some people do get divorced without making sufficient effort to resolve the situation but I also know that sometimes this is not possible and I believe that people should have another opportunity at happiness.

This is a good answer with a range of supported views. Also the candidate has given a thoughtful response of their own.

C   **'In a Christian family men and women should always be treated equally.' Do you agree? Give reasons to support your answer, and show you have thought about different points of view.**

There are different views in the Bible about the relationship between men and women in a marriage. Some people believe that, particularly in the Old Testament, women are seen as secondary to men. Some Christians say that, in the New Testament, teachings about the relationship between men and women are different. Jesus appears to treat men and women equally and has close friends who are women. However, in other places Paul, in particular, seems to be saying that women should be subservient to men. However, in the letter to the Galatians he seems to be saying that men and women are equal 'in Christ'.

In the Bible, there are different views about the relationship between men and women in married life, so Christians have different views about it. Some Christians believe that the man should be the head of the household, because there is teaching in some of the New Testament letters saying that wives should submit to their husbands. Others believe that all people are equal (Galatians) and that there doesn't need to be one 'leader' in a family, everyone should share decisions.

I believe that men and women must be equal in a relationship and must treat each other equally. Even if the Bible does not say this I still think that in the twenty-first century it is wrong for men and women to be treated differently.

This is a good answer. The candidate has shown that there is a range of teachings in the Bible and has explained these. There is also a personal opinion with supporting argument.

A   Explain Christian beliefs about the origins of humanity.

There are two different accounts of creation in the book of Genesis. In the first account it says that God created humans on the sixth day of creation and then rested on the seventh. In the second account humans are the first part of creation before there are any plants or animals. Both accounts show that the creation of humanity was special and, in some way, different from the rest of creation.

Some Christians believe that the Bible stories are literally true and that everything happened exactly as it says in the Bible, though this is difficult because the Bible contradicts itself.

Many other Christians believe that the creation stories are a myth and are ways of telling the truth about God and the world but are not describing real events. These Christians do not usually have a problem accepting scientific theories of natural selection.

> *This is a good answer. The candidate has explained the difficulties involved with the two creation stories and has also explained what is meant by a 'myth'.*

B   'The media should never make fun of religion.' Do you agree? Give reasons to support your answer, and show you have thought about different points of view. You must refer to Christianity in your answer.

Some Christians might say that it is wrong to make fun of religion in the media because religion is the most important aspect of their lives. They might argue that no one would like fun to be made of their religion, so why should people make fun of Christianity?

On the other hand, many other people, including many Christians, might say that it depends on what is meant by 'fun'. Humour is an important part of everyday life and, because people who follow a religion are also human, there are occasions when humour is just a joke that people can share. Some may say that making fun of individual people and what they do is fine but that this does not include actually making fun of their religion.

I think that humour is an important part of human life but people should show respect and care when making jokes about religion.

> *This is a good answer which considers and supports different points of view and gives a well-supported personal view.*

C   'The world is ours and we can do what we like with it.' Do you agree? Give reasons to support your answer, and show you have thought about different points of view. You must refer to Christianity in your answer.

Christians believe that God put humans on the earth to look after it and that therefore they have to take care of the world. Some Christians might also say that at the time of the creation of human beings God made them stewards. This means they have a duty to take care of creation.

Some people, on the other hand, believe that people were simply placed on the world or evolved from animals and that therefore they have no more responsibility than any other life form to take care of it.

However, all people, including those with no religious belief might think that they owe a duty to future generations to make sure that the earth is still habitable.

I believe that all people have a responsibility towards the earth. I believe this because we all live on the earth and, as humans have developed differently from other animals, it is our responsibility to ensure that the earth and the plants and animals on it survive.

> *This is a good answer. The candidate has looked at several different views including a secular one and has explained and supported these as well as a personal view.*

Complete the facts

Festivals

1   Join the festival to the event it commemorates.

Name of festival	Event it commemorates
Advent	Last week in Jesus' life
Christmas	Jesus returns to heaven
Lent	Birth of Jesus
Holy Week	Holy Spirit comes to the disciples
Good Friday	Jesus' resurrection
Easter Sunday	Preparing for Jesus' birth
Ascension	Jesus' crucifixion
Pentecost	Jesus' temptation in the wilderness

Church features

2   Fill in the following table.

Feature	What is this for?
Altar	
Pulpit	
Spire or tower	
Pool in a Baptist church	

Organisations Christians might support

3   Complete the following table.

Organisation	What it does	Is it a Christian organisation? (Y/N)
Amnesty International		
The Mothers' Union		
Christian Aid		
Greenpeace		
CAFOD		
Relate		
Save the Children		
Tearfund		

Rites of passage

4   In the left-hand column is a list of items and people that can be linked to the Christian rites of passage of baptism, confirmation, marriage and funerals. Tick the correct box(es) for each item or person.

ITEM/PERSON	Baptism	Confirmation	Marriage	Funerals
Altar				
Font				
Ring				
Sacrament				
Bishop				
Water				
Godparents				
Oil				
Nuptial mass				
Priest				
Cremation				
Vows				

Medical ethics

5   Use the words below to complete the following sentences about medical ethics.

abortion   **acceptable**   **embryos**   **fertility treatment**

sanctity   **Saunders**   **voluntary**   **wrong**

When a pregnancy is ended before the baby is born, this is called an _____

When someone makes a deliberate choice to have their life ended this is called assisted suicide or _____ euthanasia.

AID and AIH are both forms of _____

The Roman Catholic Church teaches that abortion is always _____ except in cases of 'Double Effect'.

The _____ of life is a phrase which means that life is regarded as holy and sacred.

Dame Cicely _____ founded the hospice movement in the UK.

Many Christian Churches teach that using contraception is _____

Scientists are trying to find cures for Motor Neurone Disease and Parkinson's Disease by performing research on spare _____ produced during fertility treatment.

Care for the poor

6 Complete the following Biblical quotations about care for the poor:

    a No one can serve two masters. Either..., or he will be devoted to the one and despise the other. You cannot serve both God and money. (Matthew 6:24)

    _____

    b Jesus looked at him and loved him. 'One thing you lack,' he said. 'Go, sell everything you have and.... Then come, follow me.' At this the man's face fell. He went away sad, because he had great wealth. (Mark 10:21–22)

    _____

    c Blessed are you who are poor, for yours is the... (Luke 6:20)

    _____

    d As he looked up, Jesus saw the rich putting their gifts into the temple treasury. He also saw a poor widow put in two very small copper coins. 'I tell you the truth,' he said, 'this poor widow has put in more than all the others. All these people gave their gifts out of their wealth; but she out of her poverty put in....' (Luke 21:1-4)

    _____

    e On the first day of every week, each one of you should set aside a sum of money in keeping with his income, saving it up, so that when I come... (1 Corinthians 16:2)

    _____

    f For the love of money is the root of ... Some people, eager for money, have wandered from the faith and pierced themselves with many griefs. (1 Timothy 6:10)

    _____

Racial prejudice

7 True or false? Mark with a **T** or **F** in the box your answer to the following questions.

    a Jesus told the parable of the Good Samaritan to answer the question: 'What must I do to be saved?' ☐

    b The quotation 'Do not mistreat an alien or oppress him, for you were aliens in Egypt.' comes from the book of Exodus. ☐

    c The parable of the Good Samaritan tells how a Jew helped a Samaritan. ☐

    d Samaritans were disliked in Jesus' time because they were foreigners. ☐

    e Martin Luther King Jr. made a famous speech where he said 'I have a dream...' ☐

    f Martin Luther King Jr. led the anti-slavery movement. ☐

    g Trevor Huddleston was the founder of the apartheid movement in South Africa. ☐

    h Desmond Tutu was Archbishop of Cape Town. ☐

War and peace

8 Match the descriptions in the left-hand column of the table with the words below.

boycott   **St Thomas Aquinas**   **Martin Luther King Jr.**

Religious Society of Friends (Quakers)   **conscientious objectors**

A Christian denomination that is pacifist	
He first wrote about the conditions for a Just War	
People who believe that their consciences tell them not to fight	
A type of non-violent protest	
A famous Christian who was also a pacifist	

9 Here are some of the conditions given for a Just War. What are the others?

a The war must be declared by a proper government authority.

b There must be a good reason for the war to take place.

c The war must do more good than harm.

d The methods used must be fair.

e _____

f _____

g _____

Historical figures

10 Fill in the following table.

Name	What did they do?
Amos	
Charles Darwin	
Cicely Saunders	
Jesus	
Martin Luther King Jr.	
Pope Paul VI	
Thomas Aquinas	
Trevor Huddleston	

Answers to practice questions

The Nature of God and the Trinity

1 That God has three persons: Father, Son and Holy Spirit but that they are all part of the same one God.

2 The Bible says that God created human beings in his image and many women have said that therefore God should be though of as female as well as male.

3 It does not matter which attribute you choose but it is important that you give reasons for your choice.

The Bible

1 Christians believe that the Bible is the 'Word of God'. Some people think that every word of the Bible is true and cannot be changed. Others believe that it needs to be interpreted for modern times.

2 The Old Testament contains the books of the Jewish scriptures, the Tenakh, while the New Testament is about the life and teachings of Jesus and the early church.

Jesus

1 He had a human mother, Mary, but his father was God.

2 That people should treat everyone as if they were their neighbour.

The Ten Commandments

1 So that they knew how God wanted them to live and so that he would be pleased with his people and take care of them.

2 Because it reminds people that every week they should have a day of rest when they can concentrate on God. It recalls the teaching that, after the creation of the world, God rested on the seventh day.

The Sermon on the Mount

1 Because it was the only prayer that they needed and that they should use it rather than praying in public so that other people could see how holy they were.

2 He said that divorce was wrong unless the woman was unfaithful.

The problem of evil

1 You need to begin by explaining what is meant by the problem of evil. You are asked for the ways in which Christians have tried to find an answer to the problem not your own ideas. You might say that some non-believers question that if God is all-good and all-powerful then there should be no evil in the world. You could say that the Chrirtian response could be that Adam and Eve introduced evil into the world and therefore it is nothing to do with God. Another view could be that the fact that people have the power to choose between good and evil means that people learn how to live properly.

2 The question asks you to explain Biblical teaching and you should limit your answer to this. You should restrict your answer to different Biblical examples rather than giving your own view. There are a number of examples which you can use such as the Fall in the Garden and the beginning of Original Sin, the sufferings found in the book of Job and the Devil tempting Jesus in the wilderness. As well as this, you should write about Jesus and his concern for people who were suffering. You could also point out that Jesus came to share in human pain and suffering and was crucified in order that people could go to heaven where there is no suffering.

3 You might think about how someone would support the statement and that it is a non-religious view. You then need to give a Christian view and explain that for Christians this statement is not true and that they believe there are other explanations. Finally, you need to explain and support your own point of view.

The church – history

1 He was a Jew from Tarsus who was employed to hunt out and persecute the early followers of Jesus. In approximately 35CE, he had a vision that Jesus called him. His name was changed to Paul and he began to preach the message of Christianity throughout the Mediterranean.

2 Because there were differences over Christian teachings and because people wanted to worship in different ways.

Christian denominations

1 Because some people believed that the Roman Catholic Church in the sixteenth century was corrupt. They no longer recognised the authority of the Pope and wanted to follow their own religious leaders.

2 King Henry VIII had an argument with the Pope because he wanted to divorce and remarry, which the Roman Catholic Church would not allow. Therefore, the King made himself head of the Church.

Ecumenism

1 Some believe that women should have an equal role with men in all aspects of their religion. Others think that men and women are different and that priests should be men because the first disciples were all men.

2 A place such as Taizé or Iona where Christians from different denominations meet and worship together.

The church – buildings and features

1 The altar

2 The font is a receptacle for baptising babies. Some churches have a pool instead of a font.

3 The cross is one of the main Christian symbols, representing the cross on which Jesus died.

4 These are often seen as a sign of reaching up to God.

Pilgrimage

1 To strengthen their faith, in the hope of a cure for themselves or someone else, to visit relics of the saints, to visit places associated with Jesus.

2 Although some people like to visit certain places on a pilgrimage, others believe that a real pilgrimage is exploring their own soul and finding the right way to reach God, therefore, a pilgrimage is a journey that takes a person's whole life.

Prayer

1 Adoration, confession, corporate, intercessory, petitionary, private, public, set prayer, spontaneous prayer, thanksgiving.

2 Because it reminds them of the fact that Jesus was the Son of God but born from a human mother and shows them what a good and holy woman Mary was.

Baptism

1 Because Christians believe that Adam and Eve brought sin into the world when they disobeyed God and that everyone is born with this Original Sin.

2 Baptism takes place when someone is already an adult and people are baptised by total immersion.

Eucharist

1 'This is my body, which is for you; do this in remembrance of me: This cup is the new covenant in my blood; do this, whenever you drink it, in remembrance of me.'

2 Lord's Supper, Mass, Holy Communion, Breaking of Bread, Divine Liturgy.

3 Because Christians are united together as they share the body and blood of Christ.

Confirmation

1 So that they can be prepared for the importance of the ceremony they are going through and so that they are sure that they know the teachings of Christianity.

2 Some denominations do not have confirmation because they practise adult baptism.

3 The candidates for confirmation are questioned by the Bishop to make sure that they accept Jesus and reject the devil. Then the Bishop blesses each person by putting his hand on their heads as a sign of the Holy Spirit.

Funerals

1 As a sign of respect and sadness.

2 It reminds people that the body is unimportant and it is the soul that lives on.

Life after death

1 It is not clear whether it is a physical or spiritual life but it teaches that people who follow Jesus' teachings will go to heaven.

2 Because they do not think that everyone is ready to go to heaven when they die but they have lived good lives so they are not sent to hell.

The Christian year

1 It means that every year people have the opportunity to recall all the important events in the life of Jesus.

2 In your answer you need to explain that some people might consider that Christmas is more important because it marks the incarnation, the birth of Jesus, while others would argue that at Easter Christians remember Jesus' sacrifice on the cross.

Advent and Christmas

1 The incarnation is the birth of Jesus, when God came to earth in human form.

2 Christians do not believe that Jesus was born on 25th December — they do not know when he was born. The date was fixed in 354CE by Pope Gregory so that people celebrated Christmas at a time when, in the past, they would have celebrated pagan festivals.

Lent, Holy Week and Easter

1 Because it was the time when Jesus was crucified and came back from the dead. It showed that Jesus was really the Son of God and had the power to overcome death.

2 To try to make themselves stronger and to resist temptation. Also to show that they are sorry for their sins and are preparing themselves to remember Jesus' suffering.

Ascension and Pentecost

1 When Jesus finally left his disciples and went up to heaven.

2 A Thursday

3 A Sunday

4 Whitsun means White Sunday because of the white clothes that many people used to wear for this festival.

5 Because it was the time when the disciples received the Holy Spirit and began to preach Jesus' message to other people.

6 Acts of the Apostles

Care for the poor

1 In your answer you should try and include a range of teachings. You might refer to the writings of Amos as well as to New Testament teachings. You might say that caring for the poor and demonstrating agape also shows a Christian's love for God. Jesus' teaching of the 'Golden Rule' and the two great commandments as well as the parable of the sheep and the goats should also be included.

2 Remember that you have to give different viewpoints in answering this question. You might say that for most Christians giving time and money to help the poor is a very important part of their faith. However, you might also say that there are many other important things which Christians must do and that some people who are very old or very poor themselves might not always be able to care for the poor. Finally, remember to give your own opinion and to support it.

Christian aid organisations

1 You can choose any aid organisation providing that it is Christian e.g. CAFOD, Christian Aid or Tearfund, for example. Remember that the question asks you to explain the work of the organisation and how this work shows Christian beliefs. You might begin by explaining both short-term projects, such as disaster relief, and long-term projects such as the provision of clean drinking water. Next you need to show how the work of the organisation is based on Christian teachings of loving your neighbour and helping the poor.

2 You might say that many people would agree with this statement because they feel that poor people should work harder or that they have wasted their money on other things. From a Christian perspective you could argue that poverty is not the fault of individuals and that Jesus taught that the poor would be blessed. A Christian might also say that often poverty is the fault of other people who are greedy. Remember that you have to give your own opinion and give evidence or argument to support it.

Christian attitudes to money and wealth

1 You should include some specific examples of Jesus' teaching, such as the parable of the rich fool or the story of the widow who gave all she had. You could also give examples from the teachings of Paul. Remember that you are not being asked to describe the teachings but to explain them.

2 In your answer you need to show how the way in which Christians might use their money demonstrates their beliefs. So you might write about caring for their family, giving money to charity or helping someone else in need. You could also explain that in following their religious beliefs, a Christian, would not want to waste their money on gambling for example.

3 You might say that all people have a responsibility to care for their family and would want to put that consideration first. However, you might also say that a Christian would want to ensure that other people did not suffer from the way in which they earned their money, so they might not work in the armaments industry or in gambling. Remember that you need to give your own point of view about the statement and you have to support it.

The sanctity of life

1 In your answer you need to explain Christian beliefs about the soul. These could include: the idea that the soul is what humans share with God; the belief that people have a soul which is separate from their body and which lives on in heaven when someone dies; that animals do not have a soul, and that people receive their soul before they are born.

2 In this answer you need to show how Christian beliefs about the sanctity of life can be applied to euthanasia. You could say that if Christians believe that life is sacred, they might be opposed to euthanasia because they would consider that only God has the right to decide when somebody dies. However, you might also say that Christians would not want people to suffer and that the principle of agape might apply. You could also explain the importance of hospices.

3 This statement is suggesting that concern for another human is more important than the absolute principle of the sanctity of life. You could explain that many Christians would disagree and believe that the person should be placed in a hospice where their pain can be treated and that they should pray for them. You might say that some other Christians would want to do the most loving thing in accordance with Jesus' teaching of agape and that this might involve helping someone end their pain. Remember that you need to give your own point of view and to support it with evidence.

Contraception (birth control)

1 You should show that you know what contraception is but you are not asked to describe or list different techniques. The question is about explaining Christian attitudes towards its use. You should explain that many Christians, particularly Roman Catholics, do not accept the use of artificial contraception as it is against the teachings of Natural Law and against God's will. You could also explain that many other Christians believe that it is sensible and responsible to control the number of children they have.

2 You might begin by saying that for many Christians children are seen as a gift not a right, therefore, it is wrong to suggest that it is the right of a woman to have a child. Other Christians might say that it is the right of both the father and mother of the child to make these decisions. You might also say that some women, both Christians and non-Christians, would agree with the statement. Finally, you need to give your own opinion and support it.

Fertility treatment and embryo research

1 You might explain that for some Christians fertility treatment is welcome, because it enables many couples to have children who could not do so otherwise. These people might say that God has helped people develop scientific techniques so that such treatment is now possible. You also need to explain that many Christians, particularly Roman Catholics, believe that fertility treatment is interfering with nature and going against God's will. They say that the way in which sperm is collected is unnatural and also that it is wrong to create embryos which eventually have to be discarded or are experimented on.

2 You could say that some Christians might agree with this statement as everyone would want to bring an end to suffering if they could. However, you also need to say that many Christians, such as Roman Catholics, even though they follow Jesus' teaching of agape, believe that it is totally wrong to experiment on embryos as they became human life when they were conceived. Remember to express your own view on this and to support it.

Abortion

1 You need to explain that Christians do have different views about abortion. Often these views may be based on the point at which a Christian believes a baby receives its soul or becomes a human being. You need to explain that the Roman Catholic Church teaches that this happens at the moment of conception while some other Christians believe that this only takes place once the baby is viable and can survive outside of the womb.

2 There is no teaching in the Bible which is specifically about abortion. However, many Christians would probably use teaching about the sanctity of life based on the idea of humans being made in the image of God. They might also say that abortion is murder and that this goes against the Ten Commandments. Some Christians might use the 'Golden Rule' or Jesus' teaching of agape and say that, in some circumstances, abortion might be the kindest thing to do, this could be applied to the potential mother or to the unborn child.

3 You need to explain that many people and many Christians do see abortion as legalised murder. Many people protest against its use on these grounds. However, others would argue that the foetus is not a person and therefore abortion is not murder. Remember to give your own point of view and to support it.

Euthanasia

1 You need to explain that many Christians believe that only God has the right to decide when a life should end. Therefore, euthanasia is interfering with God's plan for that person. No-one knows what God might intend for that person in the future. However, you should also explain that some Christians do believe that euthanasia might be the most loving thing to do, particularly if the person is suffering severely and there is no real hope of the situation improving.

2 Remember to explain that there is no specific teaching about euthanasia in the Bible. Therefore, people would need to use other relevant passages. They might use Jesus' teaching on agape and say that euthanasia might be the kindest thing to do in certain circumstances. On the other hand they might use passages such as 'a time to be born and a time to die' (Ecclesiastes 3:2) which suggests that these events are decided by God and not by humans.

3 In your answer you need to consider different viewpoints. These may be different Christian views or those from other perspectives. Most Christians would probably agree with the statement however there are some who feel that the kindest and most-loving action may, in some cases, be to end a life. You need to support these views. You might also consider a non-religious viewpoint where there is no God to consider. Remember to give your own views and to support them.

The hospice movement

1 In the United Kingdom – St Christopher's.

2 You need to explain that the modern hospice movement aims to provide an alternative to euthanasia. Hospices cater for the needs of the terminally ill and are designed to provide medical support and care in a comfortable environment. The movement also aims to support the family of those who are dying.

3 In your answer you are being asked to explain why a Christian might support the work of a hospice. Of course there could be many reasons, for example perhaps a relative has recently been helped in a hospice. You might also explain that many Christians would see hospices as providing a Christian response to terminal suffering and they would want to encourage people to see what they believe is a Christian solution to ending life in dignity rather than euthanasia.

War

1 Remember in your explanation that Biblical teachings can be used to support war and pacifism. You might refer to the wars in the Old Testament which were ordered by God. However, the Old Testament also has many teachings about working for a time of peace. You might also refer to Jesus' teachings about 'loving your enemies' while also mentioning the occasion when he used violence against the money-lenders in the Temple.

2 a The war must be declared by a proper authority such as a government.

b There must be a good reason for going to war, which does not include greed.

c The intention of the war must be to do good and stop evil. Therefore, wars cannot be fought out of revenge in order to intimidate people.

d War must only be fought as a last resort after all other ways of solving the problem have failed.

e The war must do more good than it causes harm.

f The war must be possible to win otherwise lives are being risked for no purpose.

g The people involved in the fighting should not use any more violence than is strictly necessary.

3 In your answer you need to consider both sides of the argument and relate them specifically to Christianity. Obviously you do not need to try to argue against the statement. You should explain different Christian points of view such as those people who feel that there are occasions, such as a Just War, when physical violence may be necessary while also considering the views of groups such as the Religious Society of Friends (Quakers) who will not use violence under any circumstances. Remember you need to give your own point of view and support it.

Human rights

1 You need to explain the Biblical teachings which might be used in a discussion about human rights. These might include general teaching on Christian love such as the 'Golden Rule' and Jesus' two great commandments. You might also explain specific examples such as the parable of the sheep and the goats. You could also explain more general church teachings about how people should respect each other and also say that Christians believe that one of the things God will judge them on is how they have treated other people.

2 In your answer you need to mention that Amnesty International is not a Christian organisation. However, many Christians believe that its actions and the work it does to help those whose human rights are being denied is in accordance with Christian teaching. Therefore, some Christians would see it as their duty to support this type of work.

Capital punishment

1 You might say that the Ten Commandments condemn murder but there are many passages where God orders the death penalty for people who had not followed his rules. You could refer to Lex Talionis 'an eye for an eye' but if you do, you must explain that it was designed to limit revenge not encourage it. You could describe Jesus' teaching about not throwing the first stone and you might also say that teaching about love in the New Testament also stresses the need for forgiveness.

2 There are several different Christian responses to this issue. Some might say that it is only right that people who take away life should in turn lose their own life. On the other hand some people might see capital punishment in itself as no different from murder. Try to balance your answer between these different views. Remember, you also need to give your own opinion and support it.

Pacifism

1 In your answer you need to explain that Christians have differing views about the use of violence. You could use material on the Just War to show how some Christians believe that there may be occasions when violence is necessary. However, you should also give examples of groups such as the Religious Society of Friends (Quakers) and explain their views on pacifism.

2 You might begin your answer by saying that although all Christians should be peace-loving, many of them are not pacifists in the way the members of the Religious Society of Friends (Quakers) are. You might say that Jesus said things such as 'Blessed are the peacemakers' but he did not say that people should never fight. You might explain that many Christians would believe it was their duty to fight for their country and for their faith. Remember to give your own viewpoint and to support it.

Prejudice

1 If possible you should use teachings from both the Old and the New Testaments in your answer. From the Old Testament you could explain the passage from Leviticus about the treatment of aliens. From the New Testament the parable of the Good Samaritan is an obvious example but you should explain the teachings in it, not describe the parable. You might also refer to Jesus teaching on agape and the 'Golden Rule'.

2 There are many ways in which Christians might do this. You cannot write about all of them so choose some examples and explain them fully. First you might say that Christians would always try to lead by example and not be racist themselves. Some of them might join particular organisations which campaign for racial equality. They should also encourage others not to be racist. Christians might also pray for an end to racism and for strength to oppose it.

The fight against racism

1 You will not get many marks if the person you write about is not a Christian, Nelson Mandela or Gandhi for example. You could choose one of the people mentioned in this book such as Martin Luther King Jr., Trevor Huddleston or Desmond Tutu. The question also asks for 'how and why' so as well as explaining how they tackled racism you also need to write about why. This may include their personal experiences as well as their religious beliefs.

2 In some ways you may think that it is difficult to produce a different viewpoint to this one but you might discuss the word 'fight' and consider that there are different ways in which people might fight. Some people might think that physical violence is an appropriate way to tackle racism while others such as Martin Luther King Jr. would only use peaceful methods of protest. Remember that you also need to give your own opinion and to support it.

Family

1 You could start be explaining that God made Adam and Eve and told them to 'Be fruitful and increase in number' (Genesis 1:28). You need to show that you understand that Christians believe that the family is important for a stable society, and that God planned that men and women should marry and have children. You could also mention some of Jesus' teaching in the New Testament, such as when he was on the cross 'When Jesus saw his mother there, and the disciple whom he loved standing nearby, he said to his mother, "Dear woman, here is your son," and to the disciple, "Here is your mother." From that time on, this disciple took her into his home (John 19:26–27).

2 You need to consider different viewpoints when answering this question. It might seem obvious that if a child's parents are religious then they will want their children to follow the same faith. They may also believe that it is their duty to make sure their children are brought up as Christians. You could offer a different viewpoint that some people might think that it is valuable for children to discover their own way. Another view might be that trying to force children to be Christians might have completely the wrong effect. Remember to give your own view and to support it.

3 In answering this question you might choose the example given, the Mothers' Union, or you might decide to choose another similar organisation. The question does not ask for a specifically Christian organisation but you should say whether the one you have chosen is Christian or not. You must remember when you are explaining why Christians might support this work you need to give Christian, as well as other, reasons.

Gender

1 This question asks you to explain specifically Biblical teaching not later teachings from the Christian Church. You might start be explaining the teaching in Genesis about Adam and Eve and consider whether this suggest they are equal. You might choose some New Testament texts, such as the teachings in Galatians about everyone who follows Christ being equal. You might also explain some of Paul's teachings in Corinthians and Titus which suggest that men and women are not equal.

2 You might find it difficult to think of another viewpoint, as the statement may seem obvious that men and women should be treated equally. However, you might say that it is possible for men and women to be treated equally but differently. You might also say something about the question of the ordination of women. Remember to give your own point of view and to support it.

3 In your answer you are expected to explain why Christians do not all agree about the ordination of women. You need to explain the facts clearly. Many non-conformist churches have had women ministers for a long time. The Church of England now has many women priests but will not, as yet, allow women to become bishops. Neither the Roman Catholic nor the Orthodox Churches allow women to be priests. You need to explain that different churches and different groups of Christians do not agree about the ordination of women. Some say that the priest stands in the place of Jesus and a woman cannot do that, others may point out the twelve original followers of Jesus were all men. Other Christians believe that women should be ordained because there are many examples of important women in the early church and because Jesus did not appear to treat men and women differently.

Marriage and divorce

1 The statement suggests that marriage is not a permanent arrangement and this is what you are being asked to evaluate in the light of Christian teachings. One point of view is that of the Church which, based on the teaching of Jesus in the Bible, makes clear that marriage should be forever – that is, until one of the partners dies. You might also explain that all the Christian churches discourage divorce and that many will not permit a church remarriage. An alternative point of view might be a secular one which suggests that it is only sensible and reasonable to think that although people may intend to stay together forever often this does not happen for many different reasons. Remember to give your own point of view and to support it.

2 In this sort of question there are no marks to be gained by describing the ceremony. You might start with the story of Adam and Eve who, according to the Bible, God made to be a couple. You should explain that Christianity sees a married relationship as the right place in which to bring up children. Many Christians see marriage as symbolising the relationship between Jesus and the Church, also the majority of Christians see marriage as a sacrament and therefore a bond which cannot be broken.

3   You should begin by explaining that all the Christian Churches are opposed to divorce but that some of them accept that sometimes a relationship breaks down and cannot be mended. In these cases, it may seem the most Christian act for people to be allowed to marry someone else. You should also explain that the Roman Catholic Church teaches that because marriage is a sacrament the vows cannot be broken and it cannot be ended. The only way in which Roman Catholics can remarry and remain within the church is by obtaining a civil divorce and then seeking an annulment from the Church. An annulment means that it has been discovered that the original marriage was faulty, perhaps one of the partners did not understand the importance of what they were doing and so the marriage never in fact took place.

The environment

1   You could begin your answer by referring to the first creation story in Genesis where God tells Adam and Eve to fill the earth and subdue it (Genesis 1:28). You could explain that because of this story Christians believe that they have a duty to acts as stewards and to care for creation. You might also explain that many Christians believe it is their general duty to preserve the world for future generations because it was all created by God.

2   The question does not ask for detail of what an environmental organisation does but for the reasons that Christians might support this work. You could therefore explain that Christians might see this as a practical way of putting their beliefs about stewardship into action. It might also mean that they consider they are doing what they can to protect the world for future generations.

3   You might begin by saying that, for a Christian, the first part of the statement is true, however you would need to continue by discussing the duty of care which Adam and Eve were given at creation. An alternative viewpoint could be an atheist one that there is no God who created the world and therefore the only peole who can take care of the world are the human population. Remember to give your own viewpoint and to support it.

Science and religion

1   In your answer to this question you might want to consider a number of different views. Some Christians believe that the two accounts of creation in the Book of Genesis, even though they are different, prove that God created the world in seven days. Some would say that these were seven periods of time, others that they were seven days of 24 hours. Other Christians might argue that these stories are myths and that science is right in its explanation of the Big Bang and natural selection. Others take the view that science shows how and religion shows why. Remember to balance your answer and to give your own views with supporting argument.

2   In your answer, as well as saying why some people might regard parts of the Bible as myth you need to explain what is meant by 'myth' and also why some people would not regard it in this way.

Religion and the media

1   The question asks you to explain different Christian attitudes towards the media in terms of whether it has advantages as well as disadvantages. Try to balance your answer showing that people might think it has both these at the same time. Generally, Christians might see that the media is a way in which the Christian message can be spread and more people can be helped to understand it. Also, it can bring a Christian's attention to many of the problems in the world. On the other hand they may believe that there is too much sex and violence in the media and this may harm children and others.

2   Although it may not be easy to find a view to support this statement, as there are probably very few Christians who do not let their children watch the television, nevertheless Christians may have very different views about what children should watch and how much television they should watch. Some people may think that families do not spend enough time together because their children are watching television. Remember to give your own point of view and to support it.

Key terms

Most of the key terms in Christianity are familiar in English, although some come from the Greek of New Testament times and others come from Hebrew.

A

Abortion the termination of a pregnancy before the foetus has reached full-term

Advent the period beginning on the fourth Sunday before Christmas. A time of spiritual preparation for Christmas

Agape Christian love, love that is totally selfless

Altar (Communion Table, Holy Table) table used for Eucharist, Mass, Lord's Supper. Some denominations refer to it as Holy Table or Communion Table

Anglican churches whose origins and traditions are linked to the Church of England

Apostle someone who was sent out by Jesus Christ to preach the Gospel

Ascension the event, 40 days after the resurrection, when Jesus ascended into heaven (see Luke 24 and Acts 1)

Ash Wednesday the first day of Lent. In some churches, penitents receive the sign of the cross in ashes on their foreheads

B

Baptism rite of initiation involving immersion in, or sprinkling of, water

Big Bang scientific theory suggesting that the universe was formed from a massive explosion of gases

C

Christ (Messiah) the anointed one. 'Messiah' is used in the Jewish tradition to refer to the expected leader sent by God, who will bring salvation to God's people. Jesus' followers applied this title to him, and its Greek equivalent, Christ, is the source of the words Christian and Christianity

Church (i) the whole community of Christians; (ii) the building in which Christians worship; (iii) a particular denomination

Creed a summary statement of religious beliefs, often recited in worship, e.g. the Apostles' and Nicene Creeds

Crucifixion Roman method of executing criminals and traitors by fastening them to a cross until they died of asphyxiation; used in the case of Jesus Christ and many who opposed the Romans

E

Easter central Christian festival which celebrates the resurrection of Jesus Christ from the dead

Embryo research medical research which uses human embryos

Eucharist a service celebrating the sacrificial death and resurrection of Jesus Christ, using elements of bread and wine. Eucharist means 'thanksgiving'

Euthanasia 'good death'; bringing about the end of a person's life to give them a more dignified death

F

Fertility treatment medical treatment intended to help people to conceive a child

Font receptacle to hold water used in baptism

G

Good Friday the Friday in Holy Week. Commemorates the day Jesus died on the cross

Gospel (Evangel) (i) good news (of salvation in Jesus Christ); (ii) an account of Jesus' life and work

H

Heaven the place, or state, in which souls will be united with God after death

Hell the place, or state, in which souls will be separated from God after death

Holy Communion (see Eucharist)

Holy Spirit the third person of the Holy Trinity. Works as God's power in the world, and lives in Christians to help them to follow Christ

Holy Week the week before Easter, when Christians remember the last week of Jesus' life on Earth

Hospice a hospital specialising in the care of the dying

I

Iconostasis a screen, covered with icons, used in Eastern Orthodox churches to separate the sanctuary from the nave

J

Jesus Christ the central figure of Christian history and devotion. The second person of the Trinity

Just War doctrine teaching about the conditions necessary for a war to be fair and right

L

Lectern a stand supporting the Bible, often in the shape of an eagle

Lent season of repentance. The 40 days leading up to Easter

M

Mass (see Eucharist)

Maundy Thursday (Holy Thursday) the Thursday in Holy Week which commemorates the Last Supper

N

New Testament collection of 27 books forming the second section of the Canon of Christian Scriptures

Non-conformist Protestant Christian bodies which separated from the established Church of England in the seventeenth century

O

Old Testament the part of the Canon of Christian Scriptures which the Church shares with Judaism, containing 39 books covering the Hebrew Canon. Some churches also include some books of the Apocrypha

Ordination the 'laying on of hands' on priests and deacons by a bishop

Orthodox the Eastern Orthodox Church consisting of national Churches (mainly Greek or Slav), including the ancient Eastern Patriarchates

P

Pacifism the belief that violence is never right

Palm Sunday the Sunday before Easter, commemorating the entry of Jesus into Jerusalem when crowds waved palm branches

Passion the sufferings of Jesus Christ, especially in the time leading up to his crucifixion

Pentecost (Whitsun) the Greek name for the Jewish Festival of Weeks, or Shavuot, which comes seven weeks (50 days) after Passover. On the day of this feast, the followers of Jesus received the gift of the Holy Spirit

Pope the Bishop of Rome, head of the Roman Catholic Church

Prejudice making a judgement without any evidence

Protestant that part of the Church which became distinct from the Roman Catholic and Orthodox Churches when their members professed (or 'protested') the centrality of the Bible and other beliefs

Pulpit a raised platform from which sermons are preached

Purgatory in some Christian traditions, a condition or state in which good souls receive spiritual cleansing after death, in preparation for heaven

Q

Quakers (see Religious Society of Friends)

R

Racism the belief that some races are superior to and more valuable than others

Religious Society of Friends (Quakers) Christian denomination committed to pacifism

Resurrection (i) the rising from the dead of Jesus Christ on the third day after the crucifixion; (ii) the rising from the dead of believers at the Last Day; (iii) the new, or risen, life of Christians

Roman Catholic the part of the Church owing loyalty to the Bishop of Rome, as distinct from Orthodox and Protestant Churches

S

Sacrament an outward physical sign of an inward invisible grace e.g. in baptism and the Eucharist

Sanctity of life the belief that life is sacred

Selling of indulgences the Church practice of selling 'certificates' to Christians that exempted the believer from years in purgatory

Sin disobedience against the will of God; falling away from the perfection of God

T

Trinity three persons in one God; belief that God's nature has three parts: Father, Son and Holy Spirit

U

Unction (anointing of the sick) the anointing with oil of a sick or dying person

Last-minute learner

Central Christian beliefs

The nature of God and the Trinity
- Christians believe that there is only one God. They are monotheists.
- Christians also believe that God can be understood in three different ways, as the three 'persons' of the Trinity: God the Father, God the Son and God the Holy Spirit.

The Bible
- The Bible is the most important and holy book in Christianity.
- Christians believe that the Bible is the 'Word of God', and a way in which God communicates to humanity.
- Christians try to understand the messages of the Bible and to put them into practice in their daily lives.

Jesus
- Christians believe that Jesus Christ was the Son of God.
- Jesus gathered around him a group of men who are known as the Twelve Disciples. They were all working men from Galilee.
- Jesus preached in the open and attracted enormous crowds wherever he went. He performed many other miracles during his ministry in Galilee, in particular healing sick people, making the lame walk and the blind see.
- Most of his teaching was in parables. These were stories which his listeners could easily understand but which had a very important message.
- Jesus angered the Jewish authorities particularly by his teaching and the Jewish priests were alarmed by the claim that Jesus was the Messiah.

The Ten Commandments
- The Ten Commandments are ten rules which Jews and Christians believe were made by God, and given to Moses to pass on to everyone else. They are part of the 'covenant', or agreement, made between God and humanity.
1. You shall have no other gods
2. You shall not worship idols
3. You shall not misuse the name of God
4. Remember the Sabbath day and keep it holy
5. Honour your father and mother
6. You shall not murder
7. You shall not commit adultery
8. You shall not steal
9. You shall not give false testimony against your neighbour
10. You shall not covet (be envious of) your neighbour's possessions.

The Sermon on the Mount
- During his ministry, Jesus spent much of his time in and around Galilee, where he preached and performed miracles.
- Jesus often taught in parables about the Kingdom of God and about forgiveness. He delivered a sermon usually called the Sermon on the Mount when he was near to the Sea of Galilee (Matthew 5–7).
- During this sermon he taught people the Beatitudes and the Lord's Prayer.

The problem of evil
- The problem of evil questions how an all-loving and all-powerful God can allow evil and suffering to exist in the world.
- Some Christians say that evil was brought into the world when Adam and Eve first disobeyed God by eating the fruit of the forbidden tree.
- Other Christians argue that God has deliberately planned challenges and difficulties for people so that they have to make choices and so mature.
- The teaching of the book of Job is that people cannot understand what God chooses to do and that they should accept suffering without complaint.

History and Christian life

The church — history
- Jesus of Nazareth: Jesus Christ was probably born around the year 3BCE in Bethlehem in the Roman province of Judaea in what is now Israel.
- He was crucified around 30CE by the Romans.
- After his death and resurrection he ascended to heaven and his disciples received the Holy Spirit. They started to preach Jesus' teachings.
- A Jew, Saul of Tarsus, was employed to hunt out and persecute these early followers of Jesus. One day, probably in 35CE, he had a vision that Jesus called him. His name was changed to Paul and he began to preach the message of Christianity throughout the Mediterranean.
- In 392CE, the Roman Emperor Theodosius I made Christianity the official religion of the Roman Empire.
- In 597CE, Augustine came to England and brought Christianity to the country.
- In 1054CE, there was a split between the churches in Rome and Byzantium over differences in teaching. These two groups became the Roman Catholic Church based in Rome with the Pope as its head and the Orthodox Church based in Byzantium under the Patriarch of Constantinople.
- In 1534, Henry VIII made himself head of the church. This broke the ties with the Roman Catholic Church and established the Church of England.

Christian denominations

- There are several thousand different denominations in Christianity.
- All these people are Christians who believe in the Trinity and that Jesus was the Son of God.
- These are three of the main groups within the Christian Church:
  Orthodox Church
  Roman Catholic Church
  Protestant churches.

Ecumenism

- Ecumenism is the name given to the belief that all churches should try to become more united. It is a movement which encourages Christians to worship together and forget their differences.

The church — buildings and features

- There are many different types of buildings in which Christians worship.
- Some of these are called churches or chapels.
- Some buildings are very large and elaborate whilst others may be small and plain.
- The type of building often reflects the style of worship which takes place in them.
- Main features include the: altar, pulpit, font.

Pilgrimage

- For Christians a pilgrimage is a religious journey.
- Usually people travel to places that have a special holy significance for them.
- Sometimes people say that a pilgrimage is a journey within. Christians can see their lives as being a pilgrimage towards God.
- Places of pilgrimage include: the Holy Land, Lourdes, Walsingham, Rome.

Prayer

- Prayer is a very important aspect of life and worship for all Christians.
- Petitionary prayer is when people ask God for something, for themselves or for other people.
- Intercessory prayer is when people ask God to intervene in the world at a time of crisis or when people are starving or suffering because of a disaster.
- Many prayers are said to thank God for creation and for life and existence in general.
- Other prayers are to ask God's help in leading a better life.
- Sometimes people use formal set prayers, such as those found in the prayer books of the various churches.
- Many Christians pray spontaneously, taking an opportunity to speak to God.

Sacraments

Baptism

- Christians believe that, because of the disobedience of Adam and Eve in the Garden of Eden, all people are born with Original Sin.
- This sin needs to be removed before people can truly live their lives as Christians.
- In most churches this cleansing of sin takes place when a young baby is baptised.

Confirmation

- Confirmation is one of the sacraments of the Christian Church.
- The Roman Catholic Church has seven sacraments: baptism, confirmation, reconciliation, Eucharist, ordination, marriage, anointing of the sick.
- A sacrament is said to be an outward visible sign of an inward spiritual grace.
- Confirmation is a celebration of when people decide for themselves to follow the Christian faith.

Funerals

- Christians believe that death is not the end of a person, although it is the end of their life on Earth.
- Christian funerals reflect this belief. Although people are sad because a friend or relative or colleague has died, they are also encouraged to think about the promise of resurrection and eternal life made by Jesus. They are encouraged to ask for God's comfort, and to thank God for the good qualities the person had, rather than concentrating only on sadness.

Life after death

- Christians believe that when they die they will have the chance of eternal life.
- Christians believe that they may go to heaven, hell or purgatory, depending on how well they have lived on Earth.

Holy days

Advent and Christmas
- Advent is the four week period which leads up to Christmas.
- Christmas is one of the most important days in the Christian calendar.

Lent, Holy Week and Easter
- Lent is the 40 days of preparation which lead up to Easter, it also recalls the time that Jesus spent in the desert when he was tempted by the Devil.
- Easter is the most important festival in the whole of the Christian year, because is celebrates the resurrection of Jesus from the dead on Easter Sunday.

Ascension and Pentecost
- Ascension Day and Pentecost are two important events in the church calendar which take place after Easter.

Wealth and poverty

- The teaching of Christianity is that all Christians have a particular responsibility to care for the poor.
- Christianity teaches that it is wrong to hold on to riches when there are people who are hungry.
- The parables of the sheep and the goats and of the rich man and Lazarus show Christian teaching about caring for those less fortunate.
- CAFOD, Christian Aid and Tearfund are examples of Christian aid organisations which are involved in helping the poor. They provide money for long-term projects as well as emergency relief and work to help developing countries become independent and less reliant on aid.

Medical ethics

- Christianity teaches that human life is sacred because all people are made 'in the image of God'.
- The majority of Christians believe that abortion and euthanasia are wrong, because they take away human life. Some Christians think that they are acceptable in certain circumstances.
- Many Christians think that it is sensible and responsible for people to use contraception. However, the Roman Catholic Church teaches that artificial methods of contraception are wrong because they go against 'natural law'.
- Some Christians approve of the use of fertility treatment but others do not because it almost inevitably means that some human embryos are destroyed.

War, peace and justice

- Thomas Aquinas wrote the conditions for a Just War.
- Some Christians are pacifists and believe that it is always wrong to use violence. The Religious Society of Friends (Quakers) are pacifists.
- Conscientious objectors believe that it is always wrong to fight in wars.
- Christians have different views about whether it is right to fight in a war.
- Biblical teaching can be found which appears to support different views.
- According to the Bible all people are made in the image of God and therefore all have value.
- Jesus taught that Christians should treat other people as they would like to be treated themselves.
- The parable of the Good Samaritan is a often used as an example of Christian teaching about prejudice.
- Trevor Huddleston, Martin Luther King Jr. and Desmond Tutu are examples of Christians who have worked to stop racism.

Family, relationships and gender

- Christians believe that marriage should always be for life. Some Christian churches do allow the remarriage of divorced people but the Roman Catholic Church only allows this after an annulment.
- Relate is a non-religious organisation which tries to help people who have problems in their relationships, and some Christians might support it.
- The Church teaches that the family has an important part to play in Christian life: it is a source of love, education and stability.
- The Mothers' Union is a Christian organisation which works to support family life.
- The Bible teaches that God made the two sexes so that they could join together in life-long partnership.
- Most Christians believe that when a man and a woman are joined together in marriage, this is a sacrament which should not be broken.
- Most Christians believe that men and women should have equal rights, responsibilities and opportunities. However, some think that men should have a leadership role and women should have a caring role.

Global issues

The environment
- The Bible teaches that the world is God's creation.
- Christians believe that they have a particular responsibility to look after the planet because God told people to be 'stewards' of the earth.

Science and religion
- Most Christians believe that scientific theories, such as the Big Bang and Darwin's theory of natural selection, are correct even though they appear to contradict the Bible.
- Some other Christians believe that the Bible is the 'Word of God' and that it is science which is wrong.

Religion and the media
- Christians do not normally object to portrayals of Jesus and other religious figures in the media.
- Some Christians believe that the media can sometimes undermine Christian values in the way in which violence, sex or marriage problems are portrayed.

Acknowledgements

Every effort has been made to trace the copyright holders of the material used in this book.
If, however, any ommissions have been made, we would be happy to rectify this. Please contact us at the address on the title page. We would like to thank the following:

Alessandro di Meo/epa/Corbis, p16; John Stillwell/PA Photos, p17; Jom Arnold/Getty Images, p22; Robert Harding World Imagery/Alamy, p23; David Young-Wolff/Getty Images, p52; Rob Crandell/Alamy, p56; St Christopher's Hospice, p60; Nick Cobbling/Alamy, p68; Bettmann/Corbis, (bottom) p73; Barry Batchelor/PA Photos, p77; Christian Aid, p47; Tearfund, p47; Cafod, p46; Amnesty International, p65.